EMPIRE STATE
OF
MIND

5 KEYS TO UNLOCK MENTAL TOUGHNESS

Copyright © Action Takers Publishing Inc 2025

All rights reserved. No part of this publication may be reproduced or transmitted in any form or by any means, mechanical or electronic, including photocopying and recording, or by any information storage and retrieval system, without permission in writing from publisher (except by reviewer, who may quote brief sections and/or show brief video clips in a review).

Disclaimer: The Publisher makes no representations or warranties with respect to the accuracy or completeness of the contents of this work and specifically disclaims all warranties, including without limitation warranties of fitness for a particular purpose. No warranty may be created or suitable for every situation. This works is sold with the understanding that the Publisher is not engaged in rendering legal, accounting, or other professional services. If professional assistance is required, the services of a competent professional person should be sought.

Neither the Publisher nor the Author shall be liable for damages arising herefrom. The fact that an organization or website is referred to in this work as a referred source of further information does not mean that the Author or the Publisher endorse the information the organization or website may provide or recommendations it may make. Further, readers should be aware that websites listed in this work may have changed or disappeared between when this work was written and when it was read.

Author Info
Email: khalil@utahbasketballclub.org

Publisher Info
Email: support@actiontakerspublishing.com
Website: www.actiontakerspublishing.com

ISBN # (paperback) 978-1-956665-78-9
ISBN # (Kindle) 978-1-956665-79-6
Published by Action Takers Publishing™

Table of Contents

Dedication v

Introduction 1

Chapter 1: The Mecca of Mental Toughness — Where It All Began .. 3

Chapter 2: Mental Toughness Lesson #1 — Believe in a Vision You Can't See But Can Feel 15

Chapter 3: Mental Toughness Lesson #2 — Sacrifice the Most Valuable Thing You Have: Time 21

Chapter 4: Mental Toughness Lesson #3 — Accountability 49

Chapter 5: Mental Toughness Lesson #4 — Our Toughest Hardships Are Our Greatest Gifts 75

Chapter 6: Mental Toughness Lesson #5 — Read the Words from the Greatest Minds 121

Conclusion 147

About the Author 149

Dedication

I've been able to navigate this roller coaster of life because of some incredible people who helped build the foundation I stand on today. These men didn't just teach me the game of basketball. They taught me the game of life. From a young age, they showed me how to sharpen my skills, not just on the court but in every aspect of life. The lessons I picked up from basketball (the discipline, the accountability, the resilience) prepared me for everything that followed. Because of them, I was able to handle the weight of responsibility, first as a college student, then as a husband, and now as a father to four beautiful kids. The impact they had on me runs deep, and I want to take these first pages to honor them for the role they played in my journey.

I dedicate this book to my mentors, Bill Calhoun and Mike Senior. As a young kid unsure of where life would take me, these two men saw something in me before I even saw it in myself. They not only taught me basketball, but they taught me how to navigate life. Their investment in me went beyond the court, giving me the most valuable tools I carry with me to this day, many of which you'll find in the pages of this book. The morals, the discipline, the lessons they instilled aren't temporary. They are lifelong, passed down through generations, because they understood that basketball was more than just a game, it was a foundation for life.

Dedication

Both of these men are true legends, men of honor who brought passion, persistence, and precision to everything they taught me on and off the court. They weren't just coaching basketball; they were teaching the game of life, molding young men like me into something greater than just players. Their commitment to their culture, their community, and to kids like me was endless. Without their belief in me, without their relentless push to make me better, I wouldn't have reaped the rewards they saw waiting for me. They knew I was capable long before I did, and for that, I owe them everything.

As my AAU coach, William "Bill" Calhoun didn't just teach me the game, he taught me how to play it the right way. When I doubted myself, he never did. He saw something in me before I saw it in myself, and because of that, he threw me into the fire. He put me in tournaments at West 4th Street (better known as "The Cage"), one of the most legendary proving grounds in NYC. He made sure I faced the best competition, forcing me to sharpen my skills against some of the toughest players in the city. Bill placed me in uncomfortable situations not to break me, but to build me. He knew that pressure makes diamonds.

I remember those practices, sweating through unbearable heat in elementary school gyms across Brooklyn, from East Flatbush to my own neighborhoods of Fort Greene and Clinton Hill. On the blacktops, the sun blazing, feet burning against the pavement, we put in work. No excuses. No complaints. Just sweat, skill, and sacrifice.

My first-ever game-winner? That happened at West 4th Street, in front of a couple hundred people watching. A moment that will forever be burned into my memory. Bill trusted me. He put the ball in my hands, gave me the green light, and let me take the shot. I haven't stopped shooting since.

The other mentor I dedicate this book to—the man I can't even begin to put into words—is Mike Senior. A true Brooklyn legend,

Empire State of Mind

raised in Brownsville, the same place that produced one of the toughest fighters of all time, Mike Tyson. And just like Tyson, Mike's coaching style was built on grit, intensity, and raw determination. And now, that same grit runs through me.

My first encounter with Mike Senior came when I played in his legendary Selvyn Smith Tournament, a proving ground for real hoopers. This wasn't some soft, organized league. This was the trenches. I found myself playing in Lafayette Gardens Projects (LG) in Bed-Stuy, one of the toughest neighborhoods in Brooklyn. You had to earn respect on that court, and nothing was given.

That's where I got the chance to be coached by another NYC legend, Kurt Smalls, a guy who made his name in Australian pro leagues but never forgot where he came from, LG. He ran the court with that same Brooklyn toughness, and I was lucky to learn under his watch.

I stood out for more than just my game; I was the only white kid out there. But that didn't matter. I didn't back down, didn't shy away from the competition. I came to prove I belonged, and that's exactly what I did. On that court, it wasn't about color; it was about heart. And I made sure they knew I had plenty of it.

I've seen this man literally throw hands protecting his brand of basketball. That's how much he believes in what he does. He started coaching at just 12 years old and never stopped. Now, in his 70s (or at least that's what I think, since he never tells anyone his age), he still cruises all over NYC, from gym to gym, park to park, shaping the next generation. He dedicates his life to kids who are fighting to escape the struggles of poverty, using basketball as a tool for survival and success.

Mike has coached thousands of kids, many of whom went on to play in college, become overseas pros, and even make it to the NBA. His coaching pedigree? Legendary. His knowledge of the game? Right

Dedication

up there with NBA-level coaches. But what truly makes him special is his relentless commitment to the game and to every kid who steps on the court under his guidance.

But beyond just coaching, Mike was a master at teaching the micro-skills that separated the good from the great. He saw the sacrifices I was making—the late nights, the early mornings, the obsession I had with getting better. Instead of just pushing me harder, he poured more fuel on the fire, guiding me to sharpen every detail of my game. He knew what I needed to work on, and he put me in places where I had to rise to the challenge.

One of the greatest opportunities Mike ever gave me was a chance to play in front of Hall of Fame coach Bob Hurley Sr. in the legendary St. Anthony gym in Jersey City, New Jersey. That gym wasn't just a building; it was sacred ground for high school basketball, a breeding ground for some of the toughest, most elite players in the country. The moment you walked inside, you could feel the history in the air. The gym had a 1960s or '70s nostalgia to it, old-school in every way, with a humidity that clung to you the second you walked in. You didn't just sweat while playing, you started sweating as soon as you stepped inside.

Mike gave me that shot to prove myself, and I wasn't about to waste it. I played my heart out that day. I tried to ignore the nerves, block out the pressure, and just give my opponents the business. I even remember one particular play where I crossed up my defender so bad he looked completely lost. After that, I drove left, lifted over a taller defender, and dropped in a clean left-hand finger roll. I had no idea at the time, but Coach Hurley Sr. had been watching. After the play, he turned to Mike and said, "That was a sweet move."

We started with half-court games, but as more players trickled in, we eventually started running full-court. That's when I spotted a

Empire State of Mind

middle-aged man walking in, carrying a pair of sneakers. I did a double take. My eyesight wasn't the best, so at first, I wasn't sure who he was. But when I got a better look, my heart nearly stopped.

This can't be real. Is that really him?

It was Bob Hurley Jr. My idol growing up. One of the Duke's University greatest point guards ever that I watched every time Duke played on TV. And now, he was stepping on the court. I was about to play against him. Unreal.

As nervous as I was, I knew I had to guard him. I wasn't going to back down. At first, I was terrified, but once the game started, my instincts took over. I played him just like I would play anybody else, full speed, all out. Did he get the best of me? Of course. What did you expect? I was 17, and he played in the NBA! But I held my own, and I knew I belonged on that court.

When the open gym was over, Coach Hurley Sr. pulled Mike aside and told him I was bound to be a Division 1 player. He even said he was going to get me into a top camp in the country so I could showcase my game in front of the right people.

I could barely process what I had just heard. To have one of the greatest coaches in basketball history say something like that about me? Priceless.

Mike gave me that shot. He put me in a room full of greatness and gave me the chance to prove myself against it. I'll forever be grateful for that.

I'm beyond grateful for these two men and dedicate this book to them. Their guidance, their belief in me, their relentless push to make me better all helped prepare me for this journey. But they weren't the only ones who shaped me.

Dedication

Of course, when people think of influence, they often think of parents. And without a doubt, my mom deserves a ton of credit. She raised me on her own while taking care of a large family, doing whatever it took to make sure we had what we needed. She didn't just raise me; she showed me how to handle adversity. She prepared me for the obstacles life would throw my way and helped me grow into the mentally strong man I am today.

Then there's Prentice and Sharon, my big brother and sister in every sense of the word. To my sister Sharon whom we just lost to cancer, keep smiling down from heaven. Prentice didn't just talk the talk, he walked beside me, literally. Every Tuesday and Thursday evening, when I was just a high school kid, he'd walk with me through Bed-Stuy to the Salvation Army gym, putting me in a position to run with streetball legends. I got to share the court with Ed "Booger" Smith and Anthony "Half Man, Half Amazing" Heyward, guys who made their name at Rucker Park—the most famous streetball battleground in the world. But those walks weren't just about getting me on the court. They were lessons. Conversations. Hours of knowledge being passed down.

Then there were others who left a lasting impact like Tim Shepard, who helped Bill Calhoun coach me. The many friends, the mentors, the park legends from Emerson Park, my second home. The list goes on.

I'm grateful for every single one of them. They say it takes a village, but I say it takes a circle—a tight-knit, trusted group of people willing to invest in you, push you, and believe in you when you don't yet believe in yourself. My goal is to share what they taught me, to pass down the same wisdom that helped shape me, so you can grow stronger mentally.

I hope that the love, the knowledge, and the passion they poured into me can be felt through these words. And most importantly, I hope this book reminds you that you are built for this. That you are mentally strong enough to handle the rock when life throws its hardest moments at you. And that when life puts you at the top—when you hit your highest moments—you remember what it took to get there.

Introduction

After countless moments of inspiration bouncing around in my mind, I finally put pen to paper, then fingers to keyboard, to bring this book to life. Growing up, sports were my world, from playing little league baseball on the barely visible diamonds tucked away in the city to hooping on the uneven concrete courts scattered across New York. The grind of becoming mentally tough has been nothing short of a roller coaster, the kind that takes your breath away, throws you for unexpected loops, and flips you upside down when you least expect it. And let me tell you, it's not a ride you master overnight.

Building true mental toughness is a lifelong process. It takes time, patience, and a whole lot of resilience. Yet, no matter where you are in your journey, you can start today strengthening that skill, adding to it every single day. I know what it feels like when life moves at the speed of light, when the obstacles feel never-ending, and when you suddenly lose your sense of direction, like a roller coaster hitting an inverted loop. Life has a way of making you feel like you've lost your way at the most unforeseen moments. But here's the truth: mental toughness is what keeps you on track, no matter how wild the ride gets.

Mental toughness is a lifelong lesson, one you have to keep learning, day in and day out. It's the key to fully embracing the rewards life has to offer while also standing firm against the never-ending trials that

Introduction

come your way. No one is immune to this ride we call life. Some roller coasters are smooth; others are straight-up terrifying. But no matter how steep the drop or how many loops you hit, your experience is yours—unique, personal, and something no one else can judge.

The thing about life is it doesn't always give you control. Once you jump into your seat and buckle up, you don't get to choose when the next twist hits. And while the world may try to judge you from the sidelines, they're not the ones on your ride. Even when it feels like you're moving at lightning speed, flipping upside down with no sense of direction, mental toughness is the harness that keeps you locked in. It's what allows you to fight through the chaos, to embrace both the struggles and the victories, and to keep pushing forward no matter what obstacles rise up in front of you.

CHAPTER 1

The Mecca of Mental Toughness – Where It All Began

When people hear the word *Mecca*, their minds immediately go to the holiest city in Islam—Mecca, Saudi Arabia. It's a place of deep devotion, rich history, and spiritual significance. If you understand the Muslim faith, you know that Mecca is home to the Hajj pilgrimage, a sacred obligation and lifelong aspiration for every Muslim who follows the teachings of the Prophet Muhammad. To visit this city, to stand in the place where their prophet was born, is one of the most profound experiences a believer can have.

As someone of Middle Eastern descent who practices Christianity, I have nothing but respect for my Afghan heritage, my Muslim friends, and my family members whose faith is deeply connected to this holy place. I've seen their devotion firsthand. I've felt the impact of their faith in action, and I understand why Mecca holds such weight in their lives.

Brooklyn: My Mecca of Mental Toughness

But for me, the word *Mecca* carries another meaning, just as sacred in my own journey. Brooklyn, New York, is MY Mecca. Brooklyn is the birthplace of my mental toughness, where my Empire State of Mind was forged. It was here, on the streets of Brooklyn, that I found my sanctuary, not within the walls of a grand mosque, but on the blacktops, in the alleyways, in the rhythm of a city that never stops moving. It was here that I learned what it truly meant to stand tall in the face of adversity. Brooklyn didn't coddle me. It didn't hand me success. It tested me, pushed me, and forced me to become something stronger than my circumstances.

Bridging Two Worlds

As a young man, newly married and visiting my father in Harlem, New York, I found myself in a place of both curiosity and reflection. My father was deep in the real estate world, navigating deals and investments while I was still figuring out my own identity. One of the things I looked forward to during these visits was the chance to sit and talk with my half-brother from my dad's side.

He was full-blooded Afghani, raised within a different cultural and religious world than mine. Me? I'm Afghani with a mix of Italian and Irish blood, a combination that, honestly, feels like a strange cocktail someone randomly decided to put together. But I love it. It makes me unique, and I've fully embraced that.

Growing up, I was raised by my mom and spent very little time with my dad. That was just how life played out. But as I got older, I made an effort to bridge that gap, to visit when I could, to understand that part of me that felt distant for so long. Whenever I came into town, I reached out, trying to create those opportunities to connect with my dad and the entire side of my family that I had only known in fragments.

In those moments, I began to see the parallel between my father's world and my own journey. While he built his career in real estate, investing in property and laying down foundations for the future, in my own way I was building my mindset, investing in my skills, and laying the foundation for the person I was becoming. Just like the city itself, I was learning how to navigate uncertainty, how to build something from nothing, and how to survive in a world that doesn't wait for you to figure it out.

That's the thing about Brooklyn, it teaches you how to adapt, how to move with confidence even when everything around you is unpredictable. The lessons I learned here were not just about basketball. They were about life, about resilience, about finding your footing when the ground beneath you is constantly shifting. Brooklyn was my Mecca of Mental Toughness, and it was here that I learned that survival wasn't just about getting by; survival is about thriving despite the obstacles.

On this particular visit, while my dad was caught up in his work, my brother Abdullah, my wife, and I decided to take a walk. It wasn't just about grabbing lunch; it was about connection. My wife and I wanted to get to know him better, to understand what life had been like for him, and to share our own experiences in return.

We had grown up in two completely different worlds. I was raised in poverty. He was raised in a stable, middle-class home. We didn't have the same struggles, the same day-to-day experiences, or the same memories of childhood. But we shared blood. And even though we didn't grow up in the same household, I knew there were things we had in common. We just had to find them.

We walked down Broadway in Harlem, one of the most famous streets in New York City. The energy of the city surrounded us. There were cars honking, people rushing past, the smell of food from street vendors mixing with the distant sound of subway grates shaking beneath our feet. We talked about life, about our different upbringings, about what shaped us. It felt like we had been walking for hours, completely lost in conversation.

The Mecca of Mental Toughness – Where It All Began

Then, out of nowhere, Abdullah suddenly stopped.

"Wait a minute," he said.

I turned to see what had caught his attention. To my left, barely noticeable between the towering apartment buildings, was a small mosque. Maybe 1,500 square feet at most—a space so easy to overlook that I never would have known it was there if we hadn't stopped.

Despite the constant rumble of the Harlem subway, the street vendors calling out, the chaos of city life, there was a steady flow of people entering and exiting the mosque. Muslim men and women, some rushing in, others stepping out in quiet reflection, as if they had just found a moment of peace in the middle of the storm that is New York City.

Without hesitation, Abdullah slipped off his shoes, stepped inside, and disappeared into the crowd.

I watched as he walked to the center of the mosque, found an open space, and knelt down in prayer.

Whoa! What an eye opening experience for me.

His commitment to God and himself to follow what he believes. To take a moment to recognize his blessings and pray for thanks and ask for whatever he decided at the time in the middle of a crazy New York City day in Harlem, New York, was a true testament to his spirituality.

That moment hit me hard.

I had seen faith in action before, but not like this. Not in a way that demanded everything pause, that required a level of devotion so strong that it didn't matter where he was or what was happening around him. His faith came first.

It was a humbling experience.

Because in that moment, I realized something: Mental toughness isn't just about pushing through struggle. It's about discipline. It's about standing firm in what you believe, no matter what's happening around you.

And that, right there, was a lesson I would carry with me forever.

Faith in the Unseen

On another occasion, I found myself in Harlem again one afternoon, visiting my father, a man I had only seen in fragments growing up. Our relationship was a complicated one, built on brief encounters rather than deep connections. He was a businessman, immersed in the real estate world, navigating the fast-moving, high-pressure landscape of New York property deals. My mother, on the other hand, was a warrior in her own right, raising me alone, shielding me from the full weight of our financial struggles, and teaching me resilience in ways I wouldn't fully appreciate until much later.

Faith is what pushes you forward when logic tells you to quit. It's what keeps you steady when everything around you is unstable. It's what makes you wake up every morning and fight for something, even when you don't see immediate results. Whether it's faith in God, faith in your craft, or faith in the process, it is the thing that separates those who break from those who break through.

I thought back to my father. There had been times when we sat in his office, talking about life, and in the middle of our conversation he would pause and say, "Hold on, son. I need a break."

Then, without another word, he would walk to the back of the room, unroll his prayer rug, face east, and begin to pray.

No distractions. No hesitation. Just him and his faith.

In those moments, I saw another level of discipline, one that I didn't fully understand at the time but deeply respected. It was the ability to tune out the noise of the world and focus on something greater. To surrender, even when the world demanded your attention elsewhere.

That, to me, was mental toughness. That was a strength that wasn't measured by muscles or speed, but by commitment and consistency.

Years later, as I pushed myself through hardships, both on and off the court, I held onto those moments. When times got tough, I reminded myself of Abdullah's quiet prayer in that tiny Harlem mosque, of my father kneeling in the back of his office, shutting out the chaos to reconnect with something deeper.

Because at the end of the day, mental toughness is about faith. Faith in yourself, faith in the process, faith in the unseen. And just like my brother and father, I had to find my own way to believe because without faith, even the strongest mind can crumble under pressure.

That lesson would stay with me for the rest of my life.

The Rock: Defining the Adversity We Face

In basketball, handling the ball aka the *rock* isn't just about skill; it's about control. You can't run an offense if you can't control the ball. You can't lead a team if you don't have command over your movements. And just like in life, you will fumble, you will lose control, and sometimes you will have it ripped right from your hands.

The *rock* isn't just a ball; the *rock* is adversity. It's every obstacle that comes flying at you when you least expect it. It's the rejection letter, the sudden job loss, the heartbreak that shakes your foundation. It's the sleepless nights when doubt creeps in, the days when nothing seems to go right. It's the moments that test you, the ones that demand an answer: *Will you crumble under the weight, or will you rise?*

Life's rock comes in different forms. Some examples include poverty, rejection, loss, failure. For some, it's a battle with mental health. For others, it's an injury that ends a dream, or a betrayal that shatters trust. Some people are blindsided by circumstances they never saw coming, while others are forced to carry burdens they never asked for. You can't control when the rock comes at you, but you can control how you handle it.

Brooklyn taught me that.

The courts of my neighborhood weren't just places to hoop; they were training grounds for real life. Every time I stepped onto the blacktop, I had to be ready for anything—full-court pressure, double teams, hard fouls that no ref was going to call. You either adjusted or got left behind. You either kept your composure or watched someone else take your spot. That's how it works in the game, and that's exactly how it works in life.

Because, at the end of the day, *how you handle the rock determines everything.*

The Courts That Raised Me

Growing up in Brooklyn, you don't just play basketball, you *survive* it. The game isn't just about skill; it's a proving ground, a culture, a way of life. It's where reputations are built and where the weak get exposed. If you don't have handles, you don't play. If you can't take a hit, you don't last. Simple as that.

I spent my days on the blacktop of Emerson Park, my home court, where battles were won and lost under flickering street lights. The courts there weren't just a place to hoop; they were sacred ground. You could hear the echoes of sneakers squeaking, trash talk bouncing between players, the unmistakable sound of the ball smacking against

The Mecca of Mental Toughness – Where It All Began

the pavement. This was our battleground, and the only way to earn respect was to prove yourself with every possession, every shot, every defensive stand.

Seasons didn't matter. Winters in Brooklyn were brutal, but they never stopped us. When snow blanketed the court, we shoveled it off, sometimes using whatever tools like broomsticks, dustpans, even our bare hands, anything we could find. We weren't going to let a little cold stop us from playing. Summers were just as unforgiving, the pavement so hot it could melt the soles off your sneakers. You'd be drenched in sweat within minutes, but none of that mattered. The ball bounced year-round because the hunger never faded.

New York City basketball is known for its rawness. The physicality. The relentless pace. You didn't get calls. There were no referees to bail you out. If you wanted a foul, you had to *earn* it, and even then, you might not get it. Every park had its hierarchy. The best players dominated the main courts, while everyone else fought for the right to be there. If you weren't good enough, you were stuck playing on the side courts until you proved you deserved better.

There was always a crowd, always an argument over a foul call, always someone looking to challenge you. The energy was electric, and the stakes felt high, even if it was just another day on the court. Losing wasn't just about taking an "L." Losing meant waiting hours for another chance to play. If you wanted to stay on the court, you had to learn how to adapt, how to keep your composure under pressure, how to step up when it mattered most.

And if you lost? You sat. You watched. You studied. You waited. And when your time came, you made sure you didn't waste it.

It was in these parks that I discovered resilience. It was these parks that I learned how to handle the *rock*—not just the ball, but the pressure, the expectations, the setbacks. Because in the game, just like in the game of life, if you don't control the rock, someone else will.

Basketball in Brooklyn was about survival. It wasn't about fancy gym workouts or meticulously designed training programs. It was about *real* competition. The old heads would test you, the veterans would push you, and the younger kids would try to take your spot before they even had the skills to back it up. You had to be sharp. You had to be relentless.

There were no easy games, no guarantees. You could show up one day and be on fire, dropping buckets left and right, and then the next day, you'd get locked down by a defender who was hungrier than you. The game had no mercy, and neither did the city.

But that was the beauty of it. If you could handle the pressure of playing in Brooklyn, you could handle anything. Because the lessons you learned on the court weren't just about basketball; they were about life. They were about resilience, bouncing back from failure, and staying ready so you never had to get ready.

Brooklyn made me. The courts raised me. And through every win, every loss, every moment of struggle, I learned the most valuable lesson of all:

Control the rock or let someone else control it for you.

Brooklyn, My Mecca

New York City is known as The Mecca of basketball for a reason. It's a legacy that runs deep in the veins of this city. Rucker Park. West 4th Street aka The Cage are world renowned parks that everyone in the basketball community have heard of and people from all over the world visit. Kobe Bryant, Kevin Durrant and so many NBA legends have played on these famous courts. These courts are hallowed ground, places where the game is stripped down to its purest form, where talent meets pressure, and only the strongest minds survive.

You could show up for a casual run and end up going one-on-one with a future NBA star. Or you could get crossed up by a local legend who never made it to the league but had the skill to outplay anyone. The culture, the hunger, the edge is what makes New York basketball different. It isn't just about skill; it's about *heart*.

Brooklyn, in particular, has its own rhythm. It is fast, gritty, relentless. The city itself mirrors the game—tough, unforgiving, full of life and opportunity but never handing out favors. You have to earn everything. If you could make it here, you could make it anywhere.

I saw that resilience firsthand after 9/11. The entire city was rocked to its core, broken and grieving, but New Yorkers stood back up. They found a way to push forward. That refusal to quit? That determination to keep moving? That was the same DNA that ran through every kid dribbling a ball on the courts of Brooklyn.

My Mecca wasn't just about basketball. It was about survival. It was about having the mental toughness to withstand the toughest blows and still keep going. Just like the city itself, you didn't crumble under pressure; you thrived in it.

And that, more than anything, is what Brooklyn basketball teaches you. That's why we call it *The Mecca*.

Lessons from the Rock

By handling the rock aka basketball or the hardships of life, it taught me everything I need to know about mental toughness. The parks were my classroom. The games were my lessons. And Brooklyn was my Mecca.

It was here that I learned that talent alone wasn't enough. You had to work. You had to grind. You had to take the hits and get back up. It was here that I learned that adversity wasn't something to fear but was something to embrace. That struggle wasn't a sign to stop, but a sign that you were growing.

Mental resilience is about how you respond to hardship. Life will test you, mostly when you least expect it. You might be exhausted, doubting yourself, feeling like you've already given everything you've got. And then, another challenge appears. Another setback. Another loss. That's when the real test begins. Can you get back up, dust yourself off, and keep moving? Or do you let the weight of failure keep you down?

On the court, I saw players break under pressure. I saw guys with all the talent in the world who couldn't handle adversity. The first time they missed a big shot, got benched, or lost a game they should have won, they folded. They let the doubt creep in. They stopped showing up, stopped putting in the work. Meanwhile, there were players with half their natural ability but twice the heart. They took every loss, every criticism, every bad game and used it as fuel to get better.

That's the difference. It's not just about skill. It's about *grit*.

Basketball taught me that resilience isn't about pretending things don't hurt. It's about *knowing* they hurt and choosing to fight through anyway. It's about staying in control of your emotions when the game isn't going your way. It's about adjusting when your plan isn't working and adapting when the situation demands it. It's about never letting one bad moment define who you are.

And most importantly, it was here that I learned that faith is the foundation of it all. Faith gives you purpose. It steadies you when doubt creeps in, and it fuels you when exhaustion tempts you to give up. It reminds you that no matter how tough things get, there's always another move to make, another lesson to learn, another opportunity to seize.

Mental toughness isn't built in comfort. It's built in the struggle. In the moments when you're tired, when you're hurting, when you're doubting yourself but you keep going anyway. That's when you level up. That's when you grow.

This is where my Empire State of Mind began.

This is where I learned how to handle the rock.

CHAPTER 2

Mental Toughness Lesson #1 – Believe in a Vision You Can't See But Can Feel

I recently took my four daughters to the eye doctor for their yearly routine checkup but one that always carries a deeper significance for me. Vision, both physical and mental, is something I hold in the highest regard. I know all too well the challenges of poor eyesight, and as a father, I want to ensure my children don't have to struggle the way I did growing up.

I have bad eyes. Always have. It's a trait that runs in my DNA, and unfortunately, it has been passed down to my daughters. I remember the first time I realized my vision was different from other kids. I couldn't read street signs. I had to squint to recognize faces until they were uncomfortably close. I couldn't make out the lights in the streets at night. They were nothing but distorted blurs, like a watercolor painting that had been left out in the rain. Everything was cloudy, unclear, and frustrating.

Lesson #1 – Believe in a Vision You Can't See But Can Feel

Yet, the most profound realization I've had about vision is that it isn't just about what you see with your eyes. It's about the kind of vision that extends beyond the physical and into the mental, the spiritual, the intuitive.

Seeing Beyond Sight

When I was a kid, I was given glasses through Medicaid. They were big, clunky bifocals that made me look like I was preparing to read stock market reports instead of hooping with my friends. I wore them for a few days, but that was all I could take. The second my friends saw me, it was over. The jokes came in rapid fire, and I wasn't about to be the punchline every time I stepped outside. So, I made the choice that I'd rather be blind than take that punishment.

I learned to live in the blur. I learned how to fake it. My friends would point at something in the distance and ask, *"Do you see that?"* And I'd respond without hesitation, *"Yeah."* But they always knew. *"Man, you lying."* And we'd laugh, because that was just life for me.

But as much as my physical eyesight failed me, it forced me to develop a different kind of vision, the mental kind. The kind that didn't rely on my eyes but on instinct, feeling, and an internal sense of direction.

Playing Ball with Blurred Vision

Now, imagine playing basketball like this. Imagine stepping onto a court where you can barely make out the rim, where the only thing guiding your shot is muscle memory and faith. Imagine trying to throw a pass to a teammate when all you see is movement, not detail. That was my reality.

When I played pick-up games, I had to train myself to focus on movement rather than detail. I memorized the colors of my teammates' jerseys so I could spot them in my periphery. I developed an acute sense of spacing, of timing, of movement without the need for crystal-clear eyesight.

And the craziest part? When I finally got contacts in high school and could see the game clearly, I felt different. It wasn't just about vision; it was about feel. I had trained myself to play in a way that relied on something deeper than sight. When I had clear vision, I almost lost the edge I had developed from years of playing in the blur.

This was the moment I truly understood something profound: Vision isn't about what you see. It's about what you believe.

Training the Mind to See What Isn't There Yet

Because of my vision struggles, I had to mentally see the game before it happened. I had to anticipate movements, visualize plays, and imagine what the court looked like even when my eyes couldn't confirm it. I would train by closing my eyes, forcing myself to feel every dribble, every pass, every shot. I created a vision of the game in my mind before it even unfolded.

My ability to believe in a vision that I couldn't physically see transferred into every aspect of my life.

I started visualizing more than just basketball plays. I imagined what my life could be outside of poverty. I pictured myself traveling to places I had never been. I created a vision of my future where I wasn't stuck in the same cycle I saw around me.

I didn't just wish for these things. I **felt** them before they became real.

Faith in the Process, Not Just the Outcome

This is the foundation of mental toughness. Believing in a vision before you see it. Too many people wait until they see progress to believe in

Lesson #1 – Believe in a Vision You Can't See But Can Feel

themselves. They wait until they get the job, the money, the opportunity before they allow themselves to have faith. But that's backward.

The most successful people, the ones who truly handle the rock in life, have faith in the process before the outcome arrives. They trust in the daily work, not just the end result.

When I trained late at night, alone in the dark at Emerson Park, I wasn't just shooting at a hoop. I was feeling my future. I was putting up thousands of shots in near-blackness, my only guide being muscle memory and faith. I saw myself making those shots before they went in. I saw my future before I lived it.

And that's what mental toughness is all about. Not waiting for proof but believing in the unseen.

Bringing It All Together: Your Vision, Your Power

Wherever you are in life, start working on your vision because that's what will allow you to handle the rock when life throws pressure your way. Your dreams, your future, your success all begin with what you see in your mind, not what's flashing in front of you on social media or TV. Before social media, how did people chase their dreams? It wasn't happening online. They put in the work. Success wasn't built on scrolling through someone else's highlights. Success was built through grit, discipline, and a relentless obsession with purpose.

Too many people get caught up thinking success is something they see online, but real success is measured in action and results, not likes and followers. There are millions of people thriving without ever posting about it, and you'd be shocked to know more success happens off-camera than on it. That's why your vision has to be stronger than the distractions.

Empire State of Mind

Be obsessed with your purpose. Let your vision fuel your growth. When you do, you'll start to rise because you put in the work and believed in yourself. This is a ***you versus you*** visualization. When you see it clearly in your mind, you'll naturally start taking the steps to make it real. Confidence comes from vision, and vision gives you the courage to do what most people won't.

You can change the world you reside in when you start with your vision. By being a visual giant, you will see your mental toughness grow beyond your expectation. You will begin to handle the rock better than before.

You will start dropping dimes in life like I was dropping ill-advised passes on the court when my teammates weren't ready. You have the power to do the same. You will start to build an empire state of mind with dart-like precision because of your focus on your vision.

This is how you handle the rock of life. This is how you build an Empire State of Mind.

CHAPTER 3

Mental Toughness Lesson #2 – Sacrifice the Most Valuable Thing You Have: Time

The Clock Starts Ticking

The moment you're born, the clock starts ticking. From day one, you're wrapped in love, held close by parents, guardians, relatives, and the closest of friends. You're embraced, adored, and showered with warmth. But not everyone gets that experience. Not every child is welcomed into the world with open arms. Some never feel that kind of love at all.

So if you're lucky enough to receive it, don't take it for granted. And if you have the power to give it, make sure you do. Because love is the foundation, the starting block of life.

But here's the thing, as you grow and navigate the world, the roads get rough. Raising a child, building a life, becoming your own person is not all smooth pavement. It gets bumpy. It gets gritty. It starts to

Lesson #2 – Sacrifice the Most Valuable Thing You Have: Time

look a lot like a beat-up New York City street, uneven, cracked, full of unexpected potholes.

And that's when mental toughness comes in.

The Potholes of Life

If you know New York City streets, you know they're not exactly smooth. Potholes are everywhere, and if you're not paying attention, hitting one can leave some nasty damage. Cars get wrecked, tires blow out, and the ride gets rough real quick.

That's exactly what happens in life when kids get older and start making choices. The road isn't smooth anymore. And if they're not prepared and don't have the tools to navigate those potholes, they're going to feel the impact hard.

If you've ever raised kids or watched your parents raise them, you know how it goes. Those sweet, refreshing moments of childhood don't last forever. The hugs, the bedtime stories, the endless love all start to shift. Before you know it, those moments are replaced with discipline, tough conversations, and accountability. And that's a hard transition, for both the child and the parent.

But just like a driver learns to avoid potholes, kids have to learn how to navigate life's rough patches. And that only happens through preparation, guidance, and mental resilience.

The Shift from Love to Discipline

Love never disappears, but it changes. The same parents who once couldn't put their baby down now find themselves scolding, correcting, and setting boundaries. It's not because the love is gone; it's because real love prepares you for the road ahead. And just like navigating those unpredictable streets, the ability to handle life's challenges comes from the lessons learned early on.

Mental toughness doesn't just appear one day. It's built through experience, through every obstacle faced, and through every lesson taught. And as the roads get rougher, that toughness is what keeps you from breaking down.

Because no matter how many potholes life throws at you, you have to keep driving forward.

Parents do their best to teach you about the good and the bad of life, the right and the wrong but let's be real, raising a child is no easy task. It's exhausting. It's overwhelming. And sometimes, the weight of that responsibility hits so hard that parents break down. They get frustrated, they snap, they say things out of stress, not because they don't love their kids, but because the burden is real.

And trust me, I learned that firsthand.

When my first daughter was born, I was hit with reality real quick. She was beautiful, perfect in every way but she had colic so bad that she never slept. And you know what that meant? My wife and I never slept either. It was brutal. Nights blurred into days, and I remember thinking, *What the hell is this? This is parenting? This is what everyone talks about with so much joy?*

I'll never forget those 3am car rides, driving through the empty streets, just trying to get her to sleep. It was the only thing that worked. I'd be exhausted, gripping the steering wheel, hoping that the rhythm of the car would finally give us a break. But night after night, it was the same battle.

Raising a baby wasn't supposed to be this hard.

And as a dad who grew up without a dad, I had a hard time understanding how to do this. I didn't know if I was doing things right,

Lesson #2 – Sacrifice the Most Valuable Thing You Have: Time

if I was failing, or if every parent felt like this at some point. I just knew I had to figure it out.

But then, finally, after a year of colic torture, things started to change. She grew out of it, and suddenly, she was the sweetest kid. And just when we thought we had things under control, life hit us with a surprise.

We accidentally had our second child, just 16 months later.

This was a blessing in disguise. My firstborn became the best big sister you could ask for. She was protective of her sister from everything and tried to comfort her when she was sad or sick.

And in those moments, I realized something. Parenting isn't about having all the answers; it's about showing up, even when you have none.

The Moments That Stick with You

We have home videos of my daughter holding her little sister, rocking her back and forth, whispering shhh, trying to get her to sleep. Those moments stay with you. They're burned into your memory, just like the stories parents tell about when you were little. You know the ones—how you loved to eat sand, how you made a mess everywhere you went, how you bit and screamed at them when they took a toy away. The classic terrible twos. I had always heard about them, but I never really understood them until I saw them firsthand. A two-year-old, still new to the world, just trying to figure things out in their own way.

Fast-Forward to the Teenage Years

If only we could just skip ahead to the teenage years. Scratch that. As a coach, I work with teenagers every day, and I'm not sure I want to see my own kids go through what I know is coming. But there's no avoiding it.

That colic baby who once cried through the night? She's in high school now.

And now, I get it.

I finally understand the worry parents carry for their kids. The same worry my mom had for me. The constant thoughts running through my head thinking, "Who are they hanging out with? Do they have the awareness to make the right choices? Are they staying out of trouble?" And the one that really gets me, "What guy is she with?"

I know I'm not the only parent who has these thoughts. I know your parents did the same thing watching, hoping, and praying that their kid would navigate life the right way.

The Cycle Repeats

Life comes full circle. The same way my mom worried about me, I now worry about my kids. The same way I tested boundaries, they will too. It's all part of growing up. And as much as I want to protect them from every pothole in the road, I know I can't.

But what I *can* do is prepare them. Teach them. Guide them.

Parents sacrifice so much to raise us. If there's one thing I've realized, it's that being a parent requires a level of mental toughness that few other roles demand. Parents are mentally tough because they willingly sacrifice the most valuable thing we have: time.

Across the world, millions of parents and guardians spend countless hours handling the rock, doing whatever it takes to provide for their children. They tend to their physical, emotional, social, and spiritual well-being, making sure they have the foundation to grow. For the first

Lesson #2 – Sacrifice the Most Valuable Thing You Have: Time

18 years, that responsibility never stops. If you added up every second, hour, and day, the time commitment would be staggering.

In some places, the sacrifice is even greater. Parents give up more than just time. They sacrifice their dreams, their money, their health—everything—to make sure their children have a shot at something better. Some make the heartbreaking decision to send their kids away, knowing they may never see them again, just so they can have a future that wouldn't be possible otherwise.

Time: The Battle We All Face

Time is the most valuable asset we have, and it moves faster than we ever expect. Ask any adult, and they'll tell you that time flies. One day you're holding your newborn, and before you know it, they're grown. Time is a battle we all try to win daily, but no matter how much we chase it, we can never slow it down.

As kids, we don't understand this. Life feels free, easy, and endless. The biggest responsibility is going to school, maybe joining a team or a club. But not every child gets that luxury. Some kids not only focus on school, but they have to work to help their parents pay the bills. Some become caretakers for their younger siblings because their mom or dad is working two jobs just to keep a roof over their heads, and the list goes on.

The Balancing Act of Time and Purpose

Time is a double-edged sword. On one hand, you need time to survive and take care of your responsibilities, provide for yourself and your family, and handle the daily pressures of life. On the other hand, you need time to figure out your path so you can chase what you love, to build a career, to follow your passion.

Being a parent, an athlete, or working toward any goal requires this balance. The reality, though, is there is no balance. An extreme amount of time is needed to raise kids or to chase dreams. You can't avoid it. You have to lose something somewhere in order to be a great parent or in order to have a successful career. Time will need to be sacrificed in some way to be great at one or the other. That is the unfortunate reality about time. You have to sacrifice time to build something meaningful. The challenge is knowing how to use the time you have wisely.

The Power of Time

Time tells everything. It reveals our priorities, our growth, and the results of our decisions. It's also a crucial part of being mentally tough. The way we invest our time in ourselves and in others shapes the lives we build. That's why time always tells.

Every second of the day moves forward, never to return. Once it's gone, it's gone. When we're awake, time is in our hands, and how we use it determines everything. The time we sacrifice for self-improvement will eventually impact others, whether we realize it or not. Time isn't just something we pass through; time is an investment that determines the strength of our mental fortitude and our ability to withstand the trials of life.

Why Time is the Most Valuable Asset

1. You will never get it back. Once a moment is gone, there's no way to retrieve it. That alone makes time priceless.

2. Time gives you the opportunity to build anything you want. Every second is a chance to create, improve, and grow.

3. Time is endless, and with it comes endless opportunities. As long as you're alive, time is always there, waiting for you to use it.

Lesson #2 – Sacrifice the Most Valuable Thing You Have: Time

4. We only have a certain amount of time, which means we have to be intentional with how we use it. It serves as a constant reminder to focus on what truly matters.

5. Time creates scars that empower us. The lessons learned through struggles, failures, and setbacks shape us into the people we're meant to be.

This is what time does. It teaches, it builds, and it defines the path we walk. The only question is, how are you using yours?

Escaping Through Basketball

As a kid playing basketball, I didn't understand the concept of time, though I was living it. I used my time to escape the scars I was living through. I used my time to disappear from watching a mom who was lonely, who was abused, who was used, and who raised a family of fatherless children through poverty. Basketball was my way out, my way of feeling like I had control over something in my life.

I used my time on the court to remove myself from getting caught up in the drugs, alcohol, and violence that were all around me. In my neighborhood, those things were a constant presence. Though I tried to avoid it, sometimes I felt myself getting pulled in.

Getting Roped In

Growing up in an environment like that, it's almost impossible not to get roped in. Sometimes it happens on purpose, other times it's by accident. But one way or another, the streets have a way of pulling you in. I remember when I was about 12 years old, on a Halloween night, acting stupid with my friends.

In our neighborhood, Halloween was different. We didn't go door-to-door trick-or-treating. Instead, the tradition for kids like us was to steal a couple dozen eggs from the grocery store and go around different neighborhoods egging people.

It was reckless and foolish, and it was our way of feeling like we had some power in a world where we often felt powerless.

No, I'm not proud of it, but that's the reality of being a kid growing up in my neighborhood. It's not an excuse, just a fact. We did things that were reckless, foolish, and sometimes downright dangerous. On that Halloween night, we thought we were just having fun, but things took a serious turn real quick.

As we roamed the streets, we spotted someone who seemed like an easy target. If you know Brooklyn streets, you know they're not that wide. Most of them are narrow, with a one-lane road squeezed between cars parked on either side. The distance from one side of the street to the other is about the length of a bus—80 feet, maybe less.

We pinpointed our target, a guy walking along the sidewalk on the other side of the street. He looked like a bum, and in our minds, that made him fair game. We unloaded about a dozen eggs, pelting him with a flurry of hits. He started to run, trying to get away, and eventually ducked into a local shop across the street.

We thought that was the end of it.

A Moment of Fear

About 30 seconds later, he ran out of the store, and we all gasped when we saw him holding a gun. He knew it was us throwing the eggs, and without hesitation, he started firing. Panic hit instantly. We scattered like thieves in the night, running in every direction. The sound of gunfire echoed through the street as we tried to stay behind the parked cars

Lesson #2 – Sacrifice the Most Valuable Thing You Have: Time

for protection. The bullets were flying our way, and all I could think about was staying low and getting out of there alive.

It was pure chaos, and it was a moment I'll never forget.

I'm not sure how many shots rang out, but we managed to escape into a local Chinese restaurant. As young teenagers, we were gasping for air, hearts pounding out of our chests, trying to get our wits about us. It took a while to calm down, and as the adrenaline started to fade, reality started to sink in.

One of my friends suddenly said his leg was hurting. At first, we didn't think much of it, but then we looked down at his lower leg, near his calf, and saw blood soaking through his jeans. There was a slight rip in the fabric, and as we looked closer, we realized he'd been shot.

We were all shocked and completely shook. The bullet had gone through the side of his leg, slicing through the skin like a blade. It wasn't a deep wound, but it was enough to send us all into a frenzy. This wasn't just a game anymore. This wasn't just some Halloween prank. One wrong move and we could have lost him.

That moment put everything into perspective, and I'll never forget what life was really like growing up as a 12-year-old kid in the hood of Brooklyn.

Turning to Basketball

At that age, I started to get serious about the game of basketball. Looking back, I'm grateful for that, because I know my friends got into more dangerous situations like that night. While I was out playing ball, they were getting caught up in things that could have gone sideways real fast. I'd hear their stories all the time, and even though a part of me felt like I was missing out, deep down I was thankful I avoided it.

I really wanted to be there with them. But there was always something pulling me in a different direction, and I used basketball as my excuse to keep my distance. Close enough to still feel connected, but far enough to keep myself out of trouble.

I used my time to lose myself in the game that gave me more than just a mental escape. It gave me the chance to physically remove myself from a world where things could go wrong in the blink of an eye. I'd spend hours on the court, working on my handles, putting in the time, without fully understanding that all of it was going to pay off later in life.

A Chosen Family

I still hung out with my friends because they were my family. We'd been through too much together to cut ties. But my real family at home wasn't the family I wanted. Life there was not easy, and basketball became my escape, my reason to stay focused on something bigger than what I saw around me.

I loved my family, but there was too much going on at home. It made me want to withdraw, to spend little time in that apartment. I can't erase that part of my life, and I don't want to because that story is what made me who I am. What I can do is use it to empower you to better value your understanding of time better.

You might be in a similar position now. You might feel trapped, not knowing how to avoid the chaos around you. Here's the truth: you can't always avoid it. Bad times are coming for all of us sooner or later, and no one is immune. But what you can do is prioritize your time in positive things. It won't eliminate the challenges, but it can make them easier to face when they show up.

Time is something you can't avoid. You have to use it, and how you use it is entirely up to you. For me, using my time wisely as a kid

Lesson #2 – Sacrifice the Most Valuable Thing You Have: Time

was a challenge, and even now as an adult, it can still be a struggle. But basketball gave me a perspective that helped me learn how to use my time. It taught me how to prioritize the things that matter, and it gave me a way to turn my focus toward something better.

The Value of Time

Time is always in your control, even though you can't actually control it. I know that sounds crazy, but that's the reality of how it works. I can't press pause right now, and neither can you. I can't rewind to change the past, and I can't fast forward to skip ahead. What I can do is make an impact in this exact moment, right here, right now.

As I'm writing this book, I know that you could be reading it days, years, or even decades after I first put these words down. But in this exact moment, both of our times are intersecting. You're using your time to read these words, and I'm using my time to share them with you. I might be old, I might be young, or I might not be around anymore, but the point is, this moment is about how we use our time to connect, to build, to learn.

Time is what builds your worth, your success, and your relationships. The fact that you're reading this right now is a testament that you're using your time wisely and efficiently. You're investing in yourself, taking mental notes, and gathering valuable lessons to improve your life. And the ultimate way to use time is to turn it into something that pushes you forward and makes you better.

Many people believe that time is money, and while that's true to an extent, I think it goes deeper than that. Time is money in the sense that the more knowledge you gain, the more opportunities you create to earn money. But it's not just about physical money. It's about building value in a way that goes beyond the dollars we use to buy things.

You become worth more than money when you can contribute to society, not just in a monetary way, but through the impact of your knowledge and actions. The value, the influence, the ideas, the help you provide, and you bring to the world goes far beyond any amount of money.

At the end of the day, money truly isn't your worth, is it? No matter how much money you have, it doesn't create the best relationships or the most fulfilling life. What does? The intellect, the values, and the character you build with your time. If you spend your time chasing money, you'll probably make it. But the real question is, how will you sustain it?

It's about how you use your morals and values to manage that gift of money and use it to make a difference in the lives of others. I once heard a great saying: "The more money you have, the more you can give back." That's a true statement, but the underlying story is even more important. It's about how you use your relationship with time to create opportunities. Time, not money, is the ultimate resource, and how you use it will determine the impact you make.

The Sacrifice of Time

My time invested in the game of basketball was usually about five to eight hours a day, not every minute on the court, but a lot of it was dedicated to basketball. I'm not saying that you have to do exactly what I did, but what I am saying is that it takes a huge sacrifice of time to get great at something. This was what it took for me, and it might be different for others, but at the end of the day, time is the key. Sacrificing a large amount of it is what will get you where you want to go.

If you want a better future, start realizing time as a companion to your greatness.

Lesson #2 – Sacrifice the Most Valuable Thing You Have: Time

As you reflect on that, ask yourself, "What am I doing with my time?" Time can either chain you down or set you free. What I mean by "free" is freedom from the mental struggles we face. If you're not investing your time in what you love, that's where pain and mental struggles happen.

If your relationship with time isn't where it should be, you'll start to feel resentment, hate, anger, and discouragement. That's exactly how I felt when I was at home. I didn't feel love, I didn't feel wanted, and I always felt like I was a burden. When you feel that way, it's a sign that your time isn't valued, that it's being wasted, that it's not worth anything.

Finding Family on the Court

As a kid, I didn't want to feel that, and the basketball court gave me the opposite of what my home gave me. The time I spent playing, honing my skills, and becoming one with the game made me happier than being at home with my family.

The people who taught me the game and invested their time in me became my family. My time was valued by them, and I valued their time by giving my best effort every time I stepped on the court.

The Power of Obsession and Time

Time allows you to become obsessed with what you love to do. The only way to know if you truly love something is to spend time with it day after day, moment after moment. That's how you become amazing at something. But here's the thing: it's not just about putting in time; it's about using that time the right way.

If you're doing things wrong, time won't magically make it better. There are no shortcuts with time. Sure, there are ways to make things simpler, but there's no shortcut to excellence. Excellence is born from time invested, time sacrificed, and time dedicated to mastering your craft.

Time is the only source that will give you the opportunity to hold on to what you believe is important. Being mentally tough means not wasting your time on things that drain your energy and pull you away from what's dear to you. If the time you're using doesn't enhance you to be your best, then you're wasting it.

A Lesson in Friendship and Competition

Thinking back, one story that stands out in my life about this concept of time and dedication happened when I played on the same AAU team as one of my best friends from Junior High School, Jemar Coleman. We're like brothers. I was about 12 or 13 years old. Jemar was always better than me. He had a game with him, meaning the dude could flat out play.

Jemar was a walking bucket. He could score anytime he wanted, and it made me jealous. We had the same class, we walked to and from school together, and we even planned to go to the same high school. That's how tight we were.

But the truth was, Jemar had more experience than I did. He'd been playing longer, and it showed. Being in his shadow was tough, but it also pushed me in ways I didn't fully understand at the time.

A Lesson in Humiliation and Determination

It became even harder for me after an experience we had playing in a basketball tournament up in Harlem. I wasn't as good as Jemar, and I had a chip on my shoulder because I was the white, half-Afghani kid who never really fit in. I was always surrounded by my African Ameri-

Lesson #2 – Sacrifice the Most Valuable Thing You Have: Time

can brothers and was the minority in the group. I never took offense to it as I always felt like a part of my friends, but there were times I just didn't relate. It led to jokes being thrown my way as the outsider in the group, and with my lack of skill on the court, it only brought on more jokes.

Because of that feeling, I would go extra hard, not caring what others thought. I wasn't as skilled as everyone else, but I'd hustle like my life depended on it. Sometimes I'd push myself so hard that I'd lose focus, like my body and mind were on two different wavelengths.

In this particular game, our team was getting worked. We had a rough first half, but after Coach Calhoun's halftime speech, we were fired up to do better in the second half. I was playing as hard as I could, but I was extremely tired and I couldn't focus. A foul was called, and I lined up at the free-throw line. My mind was racing, and I was struggling to catch my breath.

The first free throw from the other team went up, and I was still lost in my head. When they shot the second free throw, I snapped back into hustle mode. I boxed out the shooter, grabbed the rebound, and in a daze, I dribbled once and shot a pull up jump shot and hit the sweet shot.

Then, everything stopped.

My teammates, my coach, and even the other team were all staring at me. I had just scored on my own basket.

Humiliation and the Train Ride Home

It was like one of those moments you see on Instagram or TikTok with the caption that reads, "The moment you just messed up." Except replace "messed up" with a bad word, and you get the idea.

After what felt like an eternity, my teammates started screaming at me. "Bro, you shot it in the wrong basket!" I was stunned. Coach Calhoun was livid on the sidelines, shaking his head, while the other team smirked as I had just handed them two free points.

I was humiliated, but I tried my best not to let it get to me. But it did. After we lost the game, I had to endure something even more painful—the 90-minute long train ride back to the crib (slang for apartment) in Brooklyn from Harlem. Jemar and another friend clowned me for an hour straight. It was a never-ending joke session that left me wounded. I went home feeling defeated and didn't know what to do. I wanted to quit right then and there as the humiliation was brutal.

But after a few days of trying to recover from that mental beatdown on myself and from my friends, I realized I had two choices: I could give in, or I could get going. And that's the choice we all face in life. I asked myself, "How do I become better for myself? How do I drive myself to want this if I really want this? How do I become better than them, so I never have to listen to that ever again?"

The answer was simple: time.

The Spark of Obsession

That moment sparked an obsession to put an extreme amount of time into the game. I needed to become better. I needed to become obsessed. While I was investing more time into basketball, my brother Jemar took another path. His success came fast, and he got comfortable. He had an ego, stopped working, and started hanging with the wrong crowd. The game, the girls, the attention all came easy for him, and he stopped growing.

Eventually, that path led him to some harsh places, including prison. Years later, in our early to mid-30s, I got a phone call with bad news.

Lesson #2 – Sacrifice the Most Valuable Thing You Have: Time

Jemar had suffered a stroke. He was only in his 30s. A stroke? His lifestyle had caught up to him, and I couldn't believe it. I told my wife that I had to visit him, so I hopped on a flight to see him and his parents, Tamara and Jeff Coleman (I called them Ma and Pop), who were like a second family to me.

A Visit to the Hospital

When I walked into the hospital in New Jersey, I was anxious. I didn't know what to expect. I made sure to set up a time with Ma and Pop, and when I got to the recovery floor, I told the receptionist that I was there to visit my brother. She looked perplexed because she knew Jemar was black, and here I was, fair-skinned, claiming he was my brother.

They called down to the room, and after getting the okay from Ma and Pop, I walked in. Jemar didn't know I was coming. When he saw me, his eyes went wide. He looked surprised and stopped what he was doing. You could see the joy in his eyes. With slurred speech, he yelled to the nurse, "That's my brother! Look, that's my brother," and tears started to roll down his face. I looked at Ma and Pop and they were smiling. I went over and gave them a hug.

He said, "You came all the way here to see me?"

I said, "That's what brothers do, don't they?"

I spent a couple of days visiting him, talking, and sharing memories. It was tough to see him in that state, barely able to talk, relearning how to walk and eat. But I needed him to know that he mattered to me, that I loved him, and that no matter what path he had taken, he had made an impact on my life. I provided a spark. He just kept saying, "I gotta get home. I gotta get home." I reminded him that he will.

The Turning Point

Jemar doesn't know that the harsh words and clowning session I endured that day on the court changed my life. As painful as it was, it pushed me onto a different trajectory.

We spent countless hours together on the courts at Emerson Park in Brooklyn, playing side by side during our teenage years. As much as it hurt to see him in that hospital bed, I knew he had changed me. He helped me fall in love with the game. He was part of the puzzle that led me to where I am today.

I knew what I wanted after that humiliating day. I zoomed in on what I needed to do, and I stopped worrying about what others thought. I had to take control of my life and career, handling the rock my way. No friends, no family, just my will and my time to get me where I belong.

My time determines my outcome. And that's when I learned that time had everything to do with it.

The Real Secret to Success

This is the secret to your success. Nothing more. There's no hidden formula, no magic shortcut. The real formula is simple: **time over comfort**. It's about putting time into what hurts, into what challenges you, rather than staying where you're comfortable.

The more time you spend doing the most uncomfortable things, the better you get. It's in those moments that your mental toughness is honed. It's during those times that an empire state of mind is developed and fortified. Time used wisely is mental toughness. That's what handling the rock is all about.

Lesson #2 – Sacrifice the Most Valuable Thing You Have: Time

For me, my vision of finding a way out through basketball was the only thing that was ever on my mind. Nothing else drove me. Your vision needs your time. If that isn't ingrained in your mind, you won't get what you want. You'll fall short. Success demands that kind of commitment, that kind of focus.

The Power of the Present

So what does your time look like right now? Are you sitting here, in this present moment, telling yourself that it's time to get after what you want? Because the truth is, the time is now. The visions you have are happening now.

If you envision yourself in the present, no future is possible. Sure, you can have the future in mind, but it's the work you put in today that builds that future. You don't know exactly what the future holds. You don't know how it will turn out. You have a dream, but the future is just an invisible piece of your mind.

Dreams don't come true without the present. Present time needs your present work, or the big picture never gets painted. If you're indecisive with your time, it will leave you second-guessing everything. You'll never figure out what you truly want or what you're meant to be.

Building Mental Toughness Through Time

This is the thought process behind building a mind that is tough. One of the most important pieces of mental toughness is your relationship with time. Some people say you should write down your goals and others say you should have a plan. But that's never been my style. I've never been the planning type or someone who writes down their goals. I've always been a person who lives off feeling.

That approach isn't for everyone, and that's okay. You have to find what fits you. But no matter how you approach it, it all starts with time.

Take this book, for example. I felt like writing a book; I didn't plan it. It was never a goal of mine until I went through a very difficult mental stage in my life that made me rethink and rewire my mind. I did some research on how to write a book, got my ideas down, and then just started writing. That's how this book and others were created. I just took the time to get uncomfortable and get it done.

I don't know if this book will be a bestseller. If you're reading this and it is, then I'm grateful but that wasn't the purpose. That wasn't why I wrote it. I wrote this book to make an impact and help others. My use of time made all of this possible.

I didn't do it for praise or to make others proud because I wrote a book. I did it because I felt the time was now and acted upon that. What matters is my time right now. What I'm writing at this moment is what matters for you and me. If it matters to you and you feel it deep in your bones, spend time on it. That's the importance of time.

Doing, Not Thinking

Every day, I just write. Every day, I just played basketball. Not thinking too much, just doing. That's how you use time. You don't get caught up in overthinking; you just start doing.

So how do I manage it all? As a man with a family, a wife, kids, as an educator, coach, speaker, and author? I use my time on the things I love and enjoy. I no longer waste time on anything that doesn't serve me. If something or someone brings negative energy into my life, they're no longer allowed to take my time.

If you love something, make time for it. If you love it, the importance of that time will be priceless to you. You will eliminate

Lesson #2 – Sacrifice the Most Valuable Thing You Have: Time

any and all distractions to dive into what you love to create your happiness and joy.

One thing I've learned is that you cannot balance time. There's no such thing. You will never spread your time out evenly, and that's okay. You have to know that your time needs to be spent on the most important things to you.

Don't waste it on things that don't matter, or eventually, you'll find your time to be lost.

The Two-Day Rule

A pro basketball trainer once put time into perspective for me in a way that made everything click. His name is Drew Hanlen, and he works with NBA superstars like Jayson Tatum and Joel Embiid. Drew said something simple: "Never miss two days in a row of the process to get to where you want to go."

It's such a simple concept. You don't need to write it down, and you don't need to see it on paper. It's something you just feel. If you love something, never miss time with it for two days in a row. Whether it's time spent with your family, time invested in your career, or time devoted to finding your peace, you should never miss two days in a row.

I use this as my guide, and it's been very beneficial. When I was writing this book, I made sure I never missed writing for two days in a row. That's how a book gets done. That's how you handle the rock in your life.

This is what I call an empire state of mind. This is mental toughness. This is the path to your best life, your best career, and your best self.

Staying in Motion

I've narrowed in on how to spend my time wisely, and you can do so too. Use this simple piece of wisdom, and you'll see results. Make a connection with your time. Sometimes, you'll need a day to reset, and that's okay. You do need to refuel. Just like a car needs an oil change and a tune-up, we need that kind of maintenance too.

But here's the thing, the car never stops driving. You can slow it down, you can speed it up, but it has to stay in use. If it doesn't, that's when things go wrong, and it loses its juice. It doesn't run as smoothly.

In order for us to run effectively and properly, we have to stay in constant motion. There's no replacement for time, and it's crucial that you live your life and try to enjoy it. Even when it feels like what you're doing is impossible, and your mind is telling you that you can't keep going, if you stay moving, those thoughts fade away faster.

You can do the impossible.

Writing this book felt impossible, but here we are. You're reading it. I'm enjoying this process, even if it feels tedious at times. The reward for investing this time is fulfilling, and that's what keeps me focused.

The Lesson from Basketball

Basketball workouts taught me this lesson. When you're all by yourself, exhausted, with no one watching, fighting through the pain with tired arms and a racing mind telling you to quit, that's when the best moments come out. That's mental toughness. That's handling the rock.

Doing what you love will become exhausting. There will be moments when you have to push yourself beyond your limits. It's just like lifting weights. When you lift, you tear the muscle apart so it can grow back stronger.

Lesson #2 – Sacrifice the Most Valuable Thing You Have: Time

It's the same with time. Adversity is the muscle tearing apart. Using time wisely is the muscle healing and becoming stronger.

Learning Through Adversity

As a ball player, you have to deal with adversity all the time. You're constantly being defended or finding yourself in the role of the defender. There are countless moments in a game that create pressure, and one that stands out is the pick and roll situation.

In a pick and roll, the person dribbling the ball is being defended and a teammate comes to the ball handler's aid and sets a screen to alleviate pressure of the defender so the ball handler can score or pass the ball easier. Imagine a situation where I, as a 5'10" guard, have a teammate who's 6'7" setting a screen for me. Now, let's say his defender is even taller, around 6'10", and my defender is 6'4". The two defenders decided to double-team me after my teammate set the screen. It's not an easy task for a smaller guard to escape this trapping situation. I have to locate various options in a very short amount of time to make the right decision and prevent my team from being hurt by a mistake.

At this moment, I must slow my mind down while keeping my body quick. I need to stay calm, make a decisive read, and find the right angle and spacing to make a good pass or take the right shot. Fear can't play a role here. I can't let anxiety take over, and I can't move too fast either.

To be successful in this situation, I have to put myself here often during practice so that I'm ready for this moment in a game. Not every time I face this situation will I make the right read, but if I want to be prepared, I have to practice it thousands of times before I face it on the court.

Empire State of Mind

Practice is about failures. It's about learning what works and what doesn't so that when the game comes, I'm ready. Time invested in preparation creates opportunities for success when it counts. In a game, I know I can trust my experience. Most of the time I'll make the right pass or take the right shot, nine times out of ten. Maybe even ten out of ten. As a 5'10" guard playing at a high level, I had to be proficient. I had to be nearly perfect to keep my spot.

Just like in life, things don't always go as planned. You'll face situations you've never seen before, and you might not have the right answer at the moment. But when you build mental toughness and develop an empire state of mind, you learn how to manage adversity, adapt quickly, and stay focused.

Sometimes, you have to make mistakes with your time to learn how to grow. Don't take those moments for granted. It's during those moments of failure that you see who you really are. And when success finally comes, it feels even more satisfying because you know you earned it. You learned to build mental toughness through your failures, and there's a special kind of pride that comes from knowing that.

Time as Your Ally

Remember that time is an ally, not your enemy. Sure, we all know that one day our time will run out, and it might feel like it's moving too fast. But instead of focusing on how quickly time passes, learn to relish the moments of your time. Time can be a guide when you're in the dark and a source of strength during moments of negativity.

Time is your companion. It will carry you through if you stay focused on your growth instead of your undoings. When you see time this way, it's never truly lost.

Lesson #2 – Sacrifice the Most Valuable Thing You Have: Time

Befriend your time with mental toughness. Treat it as something that supports you rather than something that's working against you. When you do that, you'll handle your rock with ease because you've learned to handle time with steadfastness.

The Pick and Roll of Life

I want you to remember this analogy when dealing with the pick and rolls of life that are bound to come your way. Life is about navigating the obstacles and making the right choices when you're under pressure.

There's a short lesson on time that I want to share. Imagine a bank that gives you $86,400 every single day. You can spend it however you want, but at the end of the day, whatever money is left is taken away. You can't save it, you can't carry it over, and you can't get it back once it's gone.

If you were given this opportunity every single day, what would you do? I'm sure you'd spend it all, right? You wouldn't waste a dime of it.

Each of us has access to this bank. But this bank isn't filled with money, it's filled with time. Every morning you're paid 86,400 seconds. Now, you're not awake for all of those seconds, of course, but every moment you're awake, you get the chance to use a lot of it.

Every night, while you're resting, a portion of that time vanishes and is lost forever. Whatever time you have while you're awake, you need to invest it into something meaningful. Why? Because that time doesn't carry over into the next day. Every morning, you open a new account of time, and if you fail to use that day's deposits, the loss is yours.

There's no interest, no overdraft, and no savings. You can't draw against yesterday or borrow from tomorrow. You must live in the present and make the most of today's deposits.

Invest your time wisely, and you'll gain the utmost in health, happiness, and success.

The Clock is Running

The clock is running. Make the most of today.

They say:

- To realize the value of one year, ask a student who has failed their final exam.
  - I know what it's like to have regret—I've quit three times in my life in basketball when things weren't going my way, and I regret them all.
- To realize the value of one month, ask the parent of a premature baby.
  - I watched my mother raise my sister who had schizophrenia, and I saw the impact that every month had on her journey as a teenager.
- To realize the value of one week, ask the editor of a weekly newspaper.
  - I've written this book, and I've been part of others, so I know how important meeting a deadline is.
  - To realize the value of one day, ask a daily wage laborer who has a large family to feed.
  - I'm an educator who works up to three jobs at once at times to support my family of six.
- To realize the value of one hour, ask lovers who are waiting to meet.

Lesson #2 – Sacrifice the Most Valuable Thing You Have: Time

- o I've waited countless times for a shot at head coaching jobs to never get the opportunity that I wanted.
- To realize the value of one minute, ask a person who has missed the train, the bus, or a plane.
  - o Missing a flight is painful, especially when all you want is to get home to your kids.
- To realize the value of one second, ask a person who has survived an accident.
  - o I was almost killed by a drunk driver, and a family member involved didn't survive.
- To realize the value of one millisecond, ask the person who won a silver medal at the Olympics.
  - o I witnessed the agony of a team we beat with .9 sec left. The agony of watching defeat isn't easy even when you're on the winning side.

Time is precious, and it's fleeting. Whether it's a year, a month, a day, or just a second, every moment matters. So make the most of the time you have.

Time is a Treasure

I've had plenty of experiences that align with these statements about time, and I'm sure you have too. The thing to remember is that time waits for no one. You must treasure every moment that you have.

Treasure it even more when you get to share it with someone special. Treasure it because you did something special with it. Time is a treasure, and that treasure is what handling the rock is all about. That's what it means to have an empire state of mind.

CHAPTER 4

Mental Toughness Lesson #3 — Accountability

You are the maestro of your life. You control your energy

If you want to build real mental toughness, you have to start with accountability. Taking ownership of your actions, your decisions, and your time is what separates those who grow from those who stay stuck. Without accountability, there's no progress. No discipline. No real success.

In basketball, accountability shows up in every aspect of the game. It's in how you prepare, how you respond under pressure, and how you handle both wins and losses. If you don't take responsibility for your role on the court, you'll never elevate your game. The same goes for life.

And when it comes to playing at a high level, accountability isn't just about individual performance; it's about understanding the bigger picture and how your choices affect the team, the culture, and the game itself.

This brings me to something that changed the way basketball was played—the rise of streetball and the AND1 Mixtape era.

Lesson #3 — Accountability

The Rise of Basketball Entertainment

When you're watching a basketball game, nothing grabs your attention more than a fast-paced, action-packed battle. A high-tempo game filled with scoring, flashy dunks, and highlight plays has people glued to their screens whether it's the TV, laptop, or whatever streaming device they use today. In this era of instant entertainment, people want excitement, and they want it fast.

That high-energy style of basketball comes straight from the streets of New York City. There's no doubt about that. Streetball culture has left its mark on all levels of the game, shaping the way basketball is played, marketed, and consumed.

As I mentioned earlier, when we talk about the Mecca of basketball, we have to talk about New York City ballplayers. They were the ones who created the highlight reel before highlight reels were even a thing. Back in the day, before social media, before YouTube, the world was introduced to New York streetball through the legendary AND1 Mixtapes.

Streetball legends from Rucker Park and courts across NYC were filmed doing unbelievable things with the basketball. These weren't just regular games. This was a show, a spectacle, something that had never been seen before. And how did people watch it? On video tapes. Yes, actual VHS tapes, those things that are pretty much extinct now thanks to modern technology. Maybe they'll make a comeback like vinyl.

At the time, people would lug around huge video cameras just to capture footage of these streetballers putting on a show. What started as raw street footage turned into a global phenomenon. The AND1 Mixtape Tour took the world by storm, traveling across the country, filling arenas, and bringing streetball culture into the mainstream.

I even had a junior high school classmate who made it onto the tour. His nickname was "The Circus," but to us, he was just Fridge. He earned a contract to tour with the AND1 Mixtape Team, and it was televised on ESPN. I remember being glued to the TV, watching every episode, completely mesmerized by what I was seeing.

This era of basketball was different. It had swagger. It had energy. It had something new that made the game even more exciting. In my opinion, the AND1 era gave basketball a lift, attracting new fans and raising the demand for more creativity, excitement, and entertainment in the game.

Witnessing Greatness on the Court

Before Fridge reached his AND1 Mixtape fame, I had the opportunity to be around another legend, Ed "Booger" Smith, one of the greatest streetball players of all time. He was the only streetball player ever to grace the cover of *Sports Illustrated*, and I happened to be in it.

I was there the day they filmed and recorded this piece of history. Streetball was exploding in popularity, and people wanted to see who could claim the title of the greatest streetball player. At that time, no one could compare to Booger.

I believe it was the summer of 1997 when the issue came out. The game took place at West 4th Street, also known as "The Cage." I was standing in the front row, watching the magic unfold. If you look at the photo inside the magazine, you can spot me. I had my glasses on, arms folded, standing behind the fence, completely locked in on what I was witnessing.

Booger was on another level. He slithered through defenders like a snake through the grass. He was elusive, sneaky and smart. He put the ball between people's legs, split double teams with ease, and made

Lesson #3 — Accountability

passes no one saw coming. The hundreds of people in the crowd were hanging on every move he made.

But my connection to Booger wasn't just as a spectator. I got to play against him and with him for many summers. I knew him very well. Prentice introduced me to him when "P" started taking me to open runs in the heart of Bed-Stuy, Brooklyn. "P" would bring his daughter Shaniece with us to tag along. That is where I got my oldest daughter's name from. I wanted to have a similar name, so I named my daughter Janiece. Shaniece was named after our late sister Sharon who is Prentice's ride or die or shall we say, in English terms, his wife. Prentice and Sharon used to take care of Booger and look after him. This connection put me in front of Booger and is the reason I got to know Booger on a personal level. We ran pickup games at the Salvation Army off Nostrand Avenue and Kosciuszko Street in this little hot and humid gym with legends of New York City coming to play constantly.

This is where I learned guarding him was impossible and knew those in the game I was watching had no chance.

He was shifty, deceptive, and made you look foolish. He would wrap the ball around your head, throw it behind your back off a dribble, make you spin around lost, wondering where the ball had gone. Every move he made was poetry in motion. His passes, as ridiculous as they seemed, were always on point. What looked impossible for most players came easy to him.

His demeanor matched his game—calm, quiet, and effortless. He never needed to say much because his game did his talking.

The Sports Illustrated title of the magazine called him "The King of the Streets," and to me, they spoke the truth.

The Art of Creativity

Watching Booger up close, what made him special was his ability to be creative with his craft. He wasn't trying to imitate anyone. His game was completely authentic. This is how he played, and no one was going to stop him from being that.

He didn't overthink. He played freely, flowing with the game as it came to him. He made decisions without hesitation, and because of that, he made everyone around him better. He was a certified pro-level player.

His legacy as a streetball legend was sealed after the *Sports Illustrated* article. He played under the biggest lights, at all the legendary tournaments in NYC, for decades. Anytime he was on the court, people showed up. They came to witness a true streetball icon put on a show.

His impact was so great that he even had a documentary, *Soul in the Hole*, that captured his journey in the game. Unfortunately, like so many others, his story didn't turn out the way he (or anyone who knew him) would have wanted. For some reason or another, the streets almost always seem to find a way to pull people in.

The Lesson in Accountability

Seeing Booger's journey up close taught me a powerful lesson that you are the maestro of your own life. No one else is responsible for how your story plays out. You are accountable to you.

Your ability to create the life you want, to handle the game (whether it's basketball or life itself) is completely in your hands. The outcome, both positive and negative, falls on you.

Holding yourself to a high standard, keeping the right demeanor, staying creative, and staying true to who you are is the formula for greatness. That's exactly what Booger did every time he stepped on the court.

It was a blessing to watch.

Lesson #3 — Accountability

The Standard of a Competitor

I spent a lot of days at the Salvation Army in Bed-Stuy during high school, playing against him. I didn't grow up with Booger, but I lived near him in Fort Greene, Brooklyn. Our neighborhood is big, and you can literally live next door and may never meet anyone. Everyone lives a high pace of life in New York City and has places to go, so staying out the way is important to know if you're an outsider.

Every time we played, Boogs held himself to a high standard, and I got to witness it firsthand. He never played to lose, and his skill wasn't just for show; it was always about winning. Everything he did on the court was natural, instinctual, and calculated to give him the best chance to win. Everyone who played with him understood that. Nobody questioned his approach because his purpose was clear, even if others didn't always see it.

He never played down to his competition, not even against me. He never took it easy. He made my life miserable on that court. He embarrassed me at times, just like he did to everyone else who lined up against him.

He was a wolf, not a dog. Calm, but when it was time to hunt, he became a different beast. He played to eat. And he did just that.

He was the ultimate competitor, and just like a wolf, he knew how to control his pack. He knew when to hunt and when to protect his own.

The Power of Self-Accountability

Mental toughness is about being the one in control of your mentality. It's about self-accountability. If you're not competing with yourself at the highest level, what makes you think you'll bring that same intensity against your opponent? And that opponent isn't other people; it's life itself.

The moment you start comparing yourself to others, you set yourself up for failure. It's not just about losing; it's about losing your mental edge. And once that edge is gone, everything becomes harder. You fail more often, and you fail harder.

Now, is failing a bad thing? No. But not learning from it is the biggest failure of all. That's what will set you back the most.

If you spend too much time focused on what others are doing instead of locking in on what you need to accomplish, it's only going to lead to frustration, heartache, and disappointment.

I believe this is what led to Booger's downfall. He gave everything to those who followed him, but the problem was, no one ever gave that same energy back to him. He lost his own self-belief, and when that happened, he turned to the streets to find it.

That's just my humble take. I'm sure he could tell his own version of how it all went down, but from where I stood, that's what I saw.

The Price of Mental Toughness

When your goal aligns with your work ethic, everything falls into place. True self-accountability comes from finding satisfaction in your own progress, not from trying to satisfy others.

When you hold yourself accountable, life becomes easier, not because the challenges go away, but because you take full control. Being the maestro of your own life means not bargaining with yourself. It means paying the full price.

Mental toughness is having the capacity to accept that price. It's about absorbing the hard path, letting it settle in your mind, and allowing it to reshape your DNA so it can push you to new horizons.

This is what I saw in Booger's journey, but it's also what I built in my own world. I refused to let anyone outwork me or dictate my life, but that didn't mean people wouldn't try to stand in my way. And I'd be lying if I said I never let them.

There were times I did, and it hurt me dearly.

The Price of Emotional Accountability

When I played Division I basketball, I had a bad coach. It wasn't the first time. I had a bad coach in high school. I had a bad coach in junior college. And every single time, I let them dictate my energy toward the game. I let it tear me apart.

With all the work I had put in, with everything I had done at every stop along the way, I never held myself accountable for my own energy. Instead of staying locked in, I made terrible decisions that ultimately hindered my career.

As much as I had learned from great players like Booger, from mentors like Mike Senior and Bill Calhoun, I lacked one thing, emotional accountability. At every level, I failed to control my emotions, and because of that, I quit.

I quit in high school.

I quit in junior college.

I quit at the Division I level.

Why? Because I allowed my personal emotions to get in the way.

Was I a great player? Absolutely.

Was I capable of playing at all these levels? No doubt.

My teammates knew it.

I knew it.

The coaches knew it.

But the truth is, I was never given honesty by my head coaches. Only lies and deception.

The Lies That Broke My Trust

- My junior college coach lied to me. He promised me a full ride and then denied it. Meanwhile, he was paying other players to play there. They got apartments, living stipends, and the perks that were never offered to me, all while I had flown 2,000 miles from home chasing a dream I worked my ass off for. That was hard to swallow.

- My high school coach threw away my college recruitment letters. My teammates literally watched him do it. He made sure I never saw my opportunities.

- My Division I coach straight-up told me, *"Some strings are shorter than others."* Assistant coaches and my own teammates believed I should have started because I was the best point guard we had. But that didn't matter to the head coach.

These stories are 100% true. And as an 18- to 22-year-old kid from a tough upbringing (without the emotional intelligence and accountability to handle things the right way) I made bad choices.

I didn't channel my energy correctly. I let the frustration, the politics, and the deception dictate my emotions instead of controlling them myself.

Did it completely destroy me? No. But these life-altering choices will always stay with me.

Learning from It All

What I've taken from those experiences is this: when things get rocky, you have to hold yourself accountable. No one else will do it for you.

Lesson #3 — Accountability

The Power of Emotional Stillness

When you lack emotional stillness, it's hard to swallow the wrongs done to you. The pain lingers. The frustration builds. But when you learn to control your emotions, you make the hard things look easier. You bounce back quicker.

When you don't get the promotion at your job, when you don't get the starting position, when you don't land the dream opportunity, you still have to own your preparation. You have to own your decisions. And, most importantly, you have to own your next steps. Because everything won't go your way. That's life. And it's on your account, no one else's. It's all about how you respond to it.

Own the fact that life is going to be unfair at many turns. The only thing in your control is where you choose to put your energy and how you decide to respond.

How you respond tells more about you than anything else.

I failed at this in the past, but I've also learned along the way.

This act of accountability is mental toughness.

Accountability is how you grow an Empire State of Mind. This is how you become successful.

Mastering Your Life Starts with You

Being the maestro of your own life comes with a lot of responsibility. Too often, people put the needs of others before their own, and while that might seem noble, it can cause internal confusion. I know because I've dealt with it firsthand.

Now, this might sound crazy, especially since so many people believe that life is all about serving others and putting others first. But I believe this actually makes things harder. Yes, life is fulfilling when you give of yourself to benefit others, but that's only a piece of the pie. You cannot truly help others if you aren't first accountable to yourself.

You have to be selfish in the right way. You have to take care of your own needs first without letting the actions of others dictate your emotions. You have to control your life before you can have a meaningful impact on anyone else's.

This means sacrificing time for yourself, making space to strengthen your mind, and not feeling guilty for prioritizing your well-being.

If you don't take care of yourself first, you'll find yourself sinking in quicksand and draining your energy to make others happy when you haven't even created that happiness for yourself.

Master Yourself First

Again, there are no secrets. If you want to find peace and sustain it, you have to spend more time working on yourself than investing in others.

If you're out here trying to change the world while ignoring your own growth trying to mold yourself into something you're not just to please everyone else, you're setting yourself up for endless misery.

You'll drift through life with no purpose.

Yes, there will be people along the way who help you, who give you guidance. But if you're not constantly redefining yourself, sharpening your own iron, then you can't sharpen the iron of others.

You won't be able to master your own skills if you're too focused on what others think about you, how they perceive you, judge you, or expect you to be. If all your energy is invested in everyone else while neglecting yourself, you'll never reach your true potential.

To be great, you have to believe in your own greatness. And the only way to discover that is to focus on you first. When you do that, everything and everyone around you will naturally follow.

Lesson #3 — Accountability

The Breakthrough of Accountability

You'll know this feeling when you reach a point where you're so locked in mentally and emotionally that nothing can shake you. When you're so skilled at what you do, your artistry isn't forced; it flows naturally. And that's because you invested in your own accountability. Many call it being in the zone. That is where we want to be as often as we can be.

There will be moments when you're in the trenches, exhausted, feeling like life isn't going your way. But deep down, something will keep pushing you forward. Why? Because you did the work inside first.

When you were beat down by negativity, when people doubted you, when life threw every obstacle in your way, you focused on you. You controlled what you could. And when you do that, something changes inside you. There's a fire inside screaming that you can't be stopped.

You'll learn not to burn yourself out but, at the same time, you'll embrace exhaustion as part of the process. And in that process, you'll create a mental monster. Even more than that, you'll become a mental genius. You'll learn how to work smarter, how to manage your energy, and who is worth working with.

When you're at your breaking point and you push for just one more rep, that's when something special happens.

I relate this to writing this book. If I can write one more page when I feel like I have nothing left to say (but somehow pull out a great message from within), then I did the work. That's pure accountability. That's what we search for.

Because when you reach for one more rep, one more step, one more push when you feel like giving in, that's when you break through.

That's how we move past adversity in life.

That's mental toughness.

That's authentic accountability.

And it doesn't come from others; it comes from within the walls of your own mind.

That is an Empire State of Mind.

That is handling the rock.

Conducting Your Own Symphony

You are the conductor of your inner orchestra. You have the instruments. You have the stage. Your journey is in your control. Stop leaving things to chance. Play your symphony how you want.

If you're waiting for people who have their own responsibilities, their own bills, their own lives to manage to help you, you're going to be waiting a long time. So long that, by the time you realize it, they'll be digging the hole you're buried in.

The reality is, very few people will help you for nothing in return. The only guaranteed return in life is what you invest in yourself.

You have the power to wave your hands and make the music play the way you want. So stop handing that power off to others. Your actions are under your control. Your energy too? It's yours to give or to keep for yourself.

The Hard Choices That Shape You

The truth is, some choices aren't easy. Sometimes you have to make painful, life-altering decisions like cutting off friends or family, leaving a toxic relationship, getting a divorce, changing jobs. These decisions that can shake your world, but if you want mental toughness and inner peace, they have to be made.

Lesson #3 — Accountability

I know this to be true in my own life. And I'm sure, no matter your age or where you are right now, your life has gone off the rails at some point. Maybe you're living in one of those moments right now as you read this.

And when these moments happen, the first thought that crosses your mind is always the same... Why?

It's a natural question.

- Why did this happen to me?
- Why is my life like this?
- Why doesn't the coach like me?
- Why didn't I get the job?
- Why do I have cancer?

The list of "Why" questions goes on for all of us.

Allowing the Pain to Exist

The first step to dealing with these "Why" questions is to let the pain and suffering happen. You can't suppress these emotions. You can't bottle them up and pretend they don't exist.

I did that for 30-plus years.

As a son of a mother who married an alcoholic and an abuser, who has five kids who are all pretty much fatherless, emotions are difficult to understand. Having a mother who survives off welfare, lives off Section 8, abused her children in some ways, as a kid I never expressed my anger. I never let out my disappointment and I never allowed myself to feel the confusion.

I was always told I had to be tough.

Empire State of Mind

But how does a child (who doesn't have the mental maturity, the emotional stability, or the understanding of what's happening in his life) just "be tough"?

I was told:

- Never cry.
- Never show emotion.
- Stand up for yourself.
- Stick your chest out.
- Don't let anyone challenge you without giving it back.

That's how you claim your territory, so to speak.

I remember one summer night in my neighborhood, hanging out with my friends on the corner right in front of the same Chinese restaurant we ran into after being shot at.

My friends and I always tried to hang out with the older kids, earning our "stripes" to be accepted into the OG (Original Gangster) crew. These were the drug dealers who were our older siblings, relatives and friends of our relatives that held down the block and neighborhood we lived in. That was the goal … to prove ourselves, to be part of something bigger. To be accepted and look cool.

One night, as we stood on the corner, the older guys started stirring things up. They instigated a situation between me and one of my boys, claiming that one of us had been talking nonsense about the other. At first, it was just words, but the tension grew fast.

Before we knew it, we were in each other's faces, heated. And of course, the older guys just pushed it further, fueling the fire, waiting for a fight to break out.

And just like that, we snapped.

Lesson #3 — Accountability

Fight or Flight

It was like our fight-or-flight instincts flipped on instantly. There was no thinking. It was just a reaction. One second we were just hanging out. The next second, we were throwing punches in the middle of the street with a crowd watching. If people had camera phones back then, no doubt it would've been all over social media.

We went blow for blow, swinging, dodging, and scrapping until we were both completely exhausted. Neither of us landed anything serious, and we walked away mostly unscathed, but that wasn't the point.

The Rage We Didn't Know How to Handle

Both of us came from homes filled with struggle. His family had people locked up in prison and his father wasn't around, just like mine.

So how do you release those scars when you grow up in an environment where rage and resentment are part of daily life? We're born into situations we have no control over, but that doesn't stop us from wanting something from life.

We want revenge.

We want justice.

We want others to feel the way we feel.

But no one teaches us how to process these emotions. So instead of controlling them, we let them control us. We let them detach us from our minds, where the brain already has a natural bias toward negativity.

Looking back now, I know this: As a teenager facing my challenges, there were moments when I wanted to do some horrible things.

The Game That Saved Me

Luckily, I had control over one thing ... the game I loved. Basketball was my way out, my way to keep my emotions from getting trapped in the cycle of hate and rage that lived inside me. It was the one thing that kept me accountable. I knew that if I made the wrong decision by letting my emotions control me instead of the other way around, I could end up just like everyone else.

And deep down, we all know this. No matter how deep we are into something, we understand what our choices will lead to. The problem isn't knowing; it's controlling ourselves. We have to hone our minds. We have to train ourselves to be accountable. You can't just hope for control, you have to actively build it.

If you own your struggles, if you tell yourself, *"This is mine. This is on me,"* that alone can help you. You can't keep it bottled up. You can't be afraid to speak about it, to share it, to release it. The things we hold inside (pain, resentment, anger) don't just disappear. If you don't release them, they constrict your life until you feel like you can't move.

Breaking the Fear of Judgment

Kids are afraid. Adults are afraid.

Afraid of what people will think, afraid of being judged, afraid of showing too much of themselves. And that fear only pulls you further and further away from who you're meant to become. At some point, you have to shed a layer of yourself in order to evolve into the next version of who you are meant to be.

That is real accountability.

When I look back at my childhood, I realize I accidentally held myself accountable. I never wanted to be home. I just wanted to hoop. I didn't have a detailed plan, I didn't map out my future. I just knew that staying on the court meant staying away from everything that could destroy me.

I know not everyone has that choice. Some people don't get an escape. I'm sure plenty of people, maybe even you, have had it even harder than I did.

But at some point in life, we all get to choose.

And I chose to hold myself accountable through the game I loved.

My ambition led me to accountability.

The Standard of Mental Toughness

With this piece of mental toughness, you start to realize that what you go through isn't always just for you. Holding yourself to a higher standard gives you the power and permission to go all in on your journey. It shifts your mind onto a path where opportunities for greatness open up in your craft and in your life.

When you learn to handle both the hard and the easy with this approach, your mind expands to see endless positive possibilities.

If you believe that hardship happens *to* you, it will eat you alive.

But if you believe that hardship happens *for* you, you'll let those tough moments correct you, shape you, and push you forward.

That is an Empire State of Mind.

And when you adopt this mindset, you start to see it in others. You begin to gravitate toward people who lift you up instead of tearing you down.

I found mentors who kept me off the street corner and showed me another way. The more time I spent away from home and off the block, the easier it was for my mentors to keep me accountable, especially in moments when I didn't yet have the ability to hold myself to the standard of excellence I expected.

That's where real growth happens.

When you and the people around you hold each other accountable to giving your best and doing the work for a better future, improvement will always be knocking at your door.

Building a Winning Culture Through Accountability

This lesson came full circle during my time as head coach of a brand-new high school women's basketball program that I had the privilege to build from the ground up. There was no history of success. No winning culture. No pedigree for greatness.

The players who joined our school saw it as a fresh start, a chance to leave their past behind and step into something new. But they had the wrong mindset. They believed that just because they were in a new environment, success would naturally follow.

Unfortunately, that's not how it works.

I remember taking the job. I actually had two interviews. I wasn't even the school's first choice for the position, even though I had previously worked with the principal, and we knew each other well.

But that didn't surprise me.

I had been in this position before. Growing up, nobody really believed in me or my work ethic except me. I knew from the start that accountability was going to be the foundation of our success. And if I was going to lead this program to the top, I had to be the example first. I had to show them what accountability looked like. I had to prove how it would be done.

Lesson #3 — Accountability

Setting the Gold Standard

In our program I taught that being on time meant being early, that being on time was already late.

I instilled in them that honesty comes first. If I wasn't honest with myself and with the program, nothing big was ever going to come from it.

I pushed the mindset that your best effort is required every single day. And if that standard wasn't upheld? We'd find ways to make sure it happened, including holding myself accountable.

This became the gold standard of our program.

Year 1 of building this culture of accountability was anything but easy. Our team was filled with mostly freshmen and sophomores, with only one senior who never touched the floor much at the varsity basketball level at her previous school.

I didn't have a single player with varsity experience. But that didn't change a thing. I never wavered. I held myself accountable just like I held my players accountable. No exceptions.

I introduced a tool called "Coach Carpet." If someone was late, if someone wasn't communicating, if someone wasn't bringing the spirit and energy our team needed, they were reminded of the goals we had set for our program by Coach Carpet.

Mental Toughness Over Physical Ability

The accountability wasn't about physical mistakes; it was about mental mistakes. Because the mind controls the body. And when you control the mind, the body follows.

Coach Carpet was a 2x4 wood board wrapped in a piece of floor carpet that players had to push the full length of the basketball court. And trust me, it burned. The lungs, the legs—it was brutal.

But that was the point.

Coach Carpet wasn't punishment. It was a reminder that if we failed to uphold our standards, there were consequences, not as a punishment, but as a tool to make us better.

We all knew our physical abilities had limits, but our minds were capable of so much more. The goal was to teach this mindset to every single player.

If I was late? I did carpets. No excuses.

If a player made a mental mistake? Carpets.

If communication wasn't where it needed to be? Carpets.

We all held ourselves accountable.

Year One: Laying the Foundation

The first year of Coach Carpet was filled with thousands of them. It became a staple of our program, a symbol of what we were building. We weren't just creating a team, we were building a culture. It wasn't easy, but it paid off. Not because of our win-loss record, but because of the improvement that came with it.

We came close to beating some of the top teams in the state stacked with Division I talent, while we had none. We started four freshmen and still gave ourselves a chance to win.

We lost more than we won, but the mindset of the girls started to shift. They came from a losing program, but now they could feel the difference. They knew something was changing.

That first year, we won five games. To some, that might not seem like much. But I can tell you, we won that season because in that final game of the year, we faced the top-ranked team in the state. A team so dominant that we had no shot. And by the first quarter, the game was already out of reach.

Lesson #3 — Accountability

But what happened next? That's where we truly won.

We were down by at least 40 points, and with two minutes left, the other team was still pressing us.

Their goal wasn't just to win; they wanted to run up the score to 100 and completely embarrass us on their senior night.

I sat on the sideline, furious. I turned to my team and told them, when this game is over, we're going straight to the locker room. No handshakes. I wasn't going to let them disrespect us like that, and I wasn't going to pretend it was okay.

After telling the team, I walked back down the sideline, still fuming, and took my seat on the bench.

Then, one of my freshmen players came and sat beside me.

"Hey, Coach, can I say something?" she asked.

Still frustrated, I said, "Sure."

She looked at me and said something that stopped me in my tracks.

"Coach, what you've taught us this season is far more important than anything. We know what they're doing is wrong. But if we walk away and don't shake their hands, we're doing exactly what they're doing. And we're better than that."

I couldn't believe it. I was speechless.

The accountability we built all season long just came to life.

My player was holding me accountable.

She was checking the leader in charge. And I had nothing to say except one thing.

"You're right."

So I took a deep breath and told the team, "Let's suck it up and shake their hands."

The game ended.

They scored 100 points.

And I held my tongue and walked through that line.

The Turning Point

The story doesn't end there. That game, that moment, was a turning point for our program.

In the offseason, something shifted. The players were committed. They showed up to everything we asked of them. We put in countless hours working on our game, refining our skills, and pushing ourselves to get better. But the most important change?

The players took ownership. They held each other accountable. They weren't just following the culture; we had built a culture where they were leading it.

I watched something incredible happen. Players started telling each other to do carpets when mistakes were made. Not because a coach told them to. Because they wanted to. Players held themselves accountable. If they made a mental mistake, they didn't wait for me or my staff to say something. They dropped down and did carpets on their own.

Nobody missed a workout. Nobody showed up late.

We had become a machine. And as the leader, my role had shifted.

I didn't have to push anymore. I just had to navigate, guide, and fine-tune.

Lesson #3 — Accountability

From Fear to Dominance

Over the next two seasons, those same freshmen who once came from a losing mindset turned into champions.

They won region titles. They beat some of the top programs in the state.

And suddenly, the fear we once carried into games was gone. Now? We were the ones teams feared. This was what we had complete control over. Our mindset.

Our girls didn't have the genetics of superstar athletes. They didn't come in as natural-born winners. But they created a superstar mindset. And that changed everything.

The Magic of Accountability

The magic of accountability doesn't happen overnight. It takes time. It's not easy.

There were plenty of hard days, tough conversations, and moments where things were said that some didn't want to hear. But we stayed patient with each other.

We stuck with the process. We fell in love with the process.

Because the truth is, everyone wants to be held accountable. Deep down, we all want to be better at something. And accountability pushes people to do more than what's expected of them.

Being patient was key. Growth takes time. But accountability demands urgency. If you let things slide for too long, it will cost you.

The lesson? Don't waste time dwelling on the mistake. Put your energy into moving forward. When you hold yourself accountable, you actually gain more freedom.

Our entire program felt that freedom. And because of it, the success showed up both on and off the court. Our players didn't just become better athletes, they became leaders. They created projects to help others, provided opportunities for those less fortunate, and made an impact beyond basketball.

What we built in three years is what we all aspire to do. And in just three years, we created something special, a culture of accountability.

The Unexpected Path of Accountability

I've learned so much about accountability from my experiences growing up as well as my time as a coach. It shaped me. It paved the way for me to step outside the box and do things I never imagined, like writing this book.

I never planned to be an author. I never set this as a goal. I was pushed to do it by the pain I've faced. Pushed by the struggles that shaped me. Pushed by the need to tell my story.

My story isn't just about basketball. It's about mental toughness. The same mental toughness that got me through life, that has carried me this far in this book, and that will push me even further.

What Booger Taught Me

Booger taught me accountability. He showed me what it looked like to let your soul be in charge of your journey. He wasn't just another streetball legend. Booger was the soul of New York City. And during my time, I was blessed to be enhanced by it.

What My Team Taught Me

My women's basketball team taught me accountability in a way I had never experienced before. They showed me that you are in charge of

Lesson #3 — Accountability

your own performance. No matter how hard things get, look inside yourself and hold yourself to a high standard, even when done wrong.

The rewards will come. Maybe not right away. Maybe not even in the near future. But when you consistently hold yourself accountable, success will find you in time.

You are the Maestro

You have to take charge of your own symphony. Never fall into the trap of just being a follower. Lead your own orchestra.

True accountability means that you don't just give orders from the top. You stand side by side with the people you lead. A leader isn't someone who just tells others what to do. A leader is someone who embodies the same standard they set for others. When you surround yourself with people who believe in that same accountability, you all rise together. And when that happens? You go beyond what you ever expected.

Whether it's in your career, your relationships, your personal growth, or your craft, you create abundance in whatever you do. You get to perform life the way you want. And it all starts with personal accountability. That's what I believe is laid out right here in these words.

Handling the rock is handling your accountability. This is mental toughness. This is having an Empire State of Mind.

CHAPTER 5

Mental Toughness Lesson #4 — Our Toughest Hardships Are Our Greatest Gifts

The Life We're Born Into

When you're born, you don't get to choose your environment.

Wouldn't we all love to be born into the best possible situation? A home with a loving mom and dad, living under the same roof. Maybe even having all the money in the world, where life is smooth from day one.

Being born into a world with no worries would be nice. But we both know that's not how it goes. The reality is, you're thrust into a world that you have no control over. You don't get a say on where you land. And even if you're born into wealth, that doesn't mean you won't have your own struggles.

The truth is, when you come into this world, your circumstances are simply your circumstances. That's it.

Lesson #4 — Our Toughest Hardships Are Our Greatest Gifts

Some people are born in Africa in situations I can't even comprehend, living in dire conditions, struggling just for food, water, and basic survival.

Some are born into communities that breed hate, where kids are taught to be violent, to hate others simply because of the color of their skin.

Some are born into middle-class homes with a single parent who can provide a comfortable life but still face challenges.

The Generational Cycle

The environments we grow up in don't just appear out of nowhere. They are passed down, generation after generation. Is it accidental? Or is it by design? I'll let your relationship with your higher power determine that.

But what I do know is that at some point these circumstances are shaped by choices. Sometimes, it's the choices of individuals. Sometimes, it's other choices that hurt you. Sometimes it's the choices of those in power, like rulers, dictators, and systems built to control people.

Whatever your view, one thing is for certain: the lives we are thrust into are built on generational habits, passed down until someone in the family decides to break the curse.

Our DNA carries our traits, our tendencies, and our habits. But the environment we're raised in determines whether those traits are enhanced for good or pushed toward negativity.

There's no way around that.

Breaking the Cycle: A Childhood of Survival

When I was born, my mother had already given birth to my older brother. He had never met his father; his dad was just gone. Then came me, and not long after, my father left too. He chose his religious obligations over my mother and me.

A single mother, raising two boys, my mother tried to hold everything together. From my perspective as a child, it didn't seem so bad. But my mother's life before me? That was far from easy. She had been adopted after suffering abuse from her biological parents. That trauma stayed with her, and as much as she tried, it came out in the way she raised us.

My mother was a calm person ... until she wasn't. She had a temper, and when it came out, it came out hard. I recognize a lot of that in myself. The abuse she endured was passed down to her. And though it hurt, I don't fault her for that.

There were times I would hide under my bed, trying to avoid the sting of a phone wire or the snap of a leather belt across my back ... all because I had misbehaved.

She wasn't a mother who had been loved; she had been abandoned by her biological parents, by my brother's father, and by my father. She had never been shown love in a healthy way, so she spent her life searching for it.

But the cycle wasn't done repeating itself. A decade later, my younger brother was born. His father ran off, too.

Then came my stepfather, a man who drank too much and could never fully be himself because of it. I watched my mother cry at night, trying to hold together a life she never expected. I watched her raise four boys with a man who was barely present, and when he was, he

Lesson #4 — Our Toughest Hardships Are Our Greatest Gifts

wasn't himself. The abuse was silent, but we all saw it. My mother chose this life, not because she wanted it, but because it was all she knew.

She didn't know any different. She was never taught a different way. Or maybe she was, but she never used it. She never had a real connection to what happiness looks like. I never saw my mother truly happy. All I saw was pain in her eyes. Frustration. Disappointment. Resentment. Anger.

More Than She Could Handle

Then, with the heart she had left, my mother adopted my little sister. By blood, she was my cousin. My aunt (who was heading down a path of drug abuse) had given birth to her, and my mother took her in. That decision came with a weight none of us were ready for. She had been born with severe mental complications due to my aunt's drug use during pregnancy. That added even more pressure to our family. It took a toll on all of us.

For me, I dealt with it by trying to please my mother. I was a mild-mannered kid and a rule follower. I just wanted to make her happy. At 10 or 11 years old, I found myself watching my younger siblings alone (sometimes for hours) with no idea where my mother had gone. I had no clue how to take care of crying babies or what they needed. I got angry. Not because I didn't love them, but because I didn't know what to do.

That wasn't even the worst part. My aunt lived in the same apartment building. I would go to see my aunt often as she lived on the top floor of the apartment right above us. I was her favorite. She gave me my nickname of "Puddy" due to my favorite cartoon show on "The Looney Tunes" with Tweety Bird and Sylvester the Cat. Tweety would say,

"I taut I taw a "Puddy" tat." I would constantly say "Puddy Cat" so my aunt decided that was my nickname. It stuck with me. There were many days I'd go upstairs to her place looking for my "TT" when my mom would ask to see if she was home. She wouldn't be there. I'd find my baby cousin, the brother of my sister who was a few years older, would be alone in his crib for hours at a time, maybe even a whole day, I truly don't know. My little soul felt something was wrong. I would find my cousin in his crib with just a bottle of apple juice and a pacifier. I'd sit there with him. I'd play with him for a while. Hours would go by, no adult around would come to his aid so I sat with him. My aunt was out in the world abusing her drugs while her children lay at home abandoned. But what could I do? I was just a kid. I'd put him back in his crib and go on with my day, not understanding the reality of what was happening.

Looking back, I wish I had known what to do. But I was just a child, carrying a weight too heavy for me to hold. And I never told anyone. I didn't want to get anyone in trouble. So I just stayed silent.

Scars That Stayed with Me

The sounds of my siblings crying for hours, my baby cousin left alone in his crib crying looking me in the eye as I left him alone—those moments never left me. And when I became a father myself, those memories made it hard for me to be present for my own kids. I buried it. I hid it. But it still affected my family. I carried resentment toward my mother for putting me in that position. I felt like I failed as a brother and cousin. Is this what family is supposed to do? I felt guilty. As a teenager, it broke me.

Looking back now, I understand my mother more than I ever did then. She had been through hell. The life she lived was always in survival mode. What I learned from her was how to survive, not how to thrive. She survived the life she was born into.

But as she got older, she started to choose differently. Was it the best choice every time? No. But was it the best she knew how to make? Yes. And for that, I'm proud of her. She is a walking testimony that you can get through the hardest things in life.

That resilience is real.

That growth is possible.

That even though we don't always get to choose where we start, we do get to choose where we go.

The Void That Shapes Us

When there's a missing piece in life, whether you believe in a higher power or not, there's a spiritual gap, unseen but deeply felt, that we all yearn for. Some call it purpose. Some call it reason. Whatever name you give it, when it's missing, life becomes harder. That was my mother's journey.

If you've seen this in your own family, you know exactly what I'm talking about. When you're missing something you desperately need, when there's a void you can't seem to fill, it's hard to face life with optimism.

Being raised without valuable relationships leaves a lot of unanswered questions. Without meaningful connections, every challenge feels heavier. That's why so many people slip into the shadows searching for something to fill that emptiness until those shadows become total darkness. It becomes a battle within your own mind, a battle that's nearly impossible to win if you're surrounded by the wrong environment. And my mother? She was surrounded by the very thing that could've consumed her.

The Avoidance That Shaped Me

As a kid, the only way I knew how to deal with it was to avoid it altogether. I reached a point where I told myself, "I don't need this" and made a choice: I will not be around my mom. When she tried to force a relationship between me and my dad (not for love, but so he would pay child support), I refused. Why? Because I remember staring out the window for hours, waiting for my dad to show up.

My mom would tell me, "He wants to see you. He's coming to spend time with you." So I waited. Four hours. Five hours. Maybe six. I'd run from watching TV back to the window, hoping he'd be there. But he never showed up.

That pain still sticks with me. Eventually, I came to a decision: If my dad's child support check was the only thing he would ever give me, then I would take advantage of it. That check gave me an opportunity. It lets me keep up with my friends. It let me finally have the newest Jordans, the freshest Ralph Lauren, and the Guess jeans. I had all the high-end clothing that everyone else had but I rarely did.

If you didn't have the latest gear, you got clowned on. For a kid like me, that check was a means to an end. When I showed up at school, everyone gave me props for the gear I was wearing, and it made me feel like I was on top of the world. I got my self-esteem from this. Little did I know, materials come and go. I built a false sense of security in myself from this. The money was incinerated by buying a sweater for $200 and shoes for $150. A $500 dollar child support check disappeared in a matter of days. Magic Money I call it. Money that disappeared as fast as you saw it.

My mom was just trying to get by on a government check at this time. I knew and didn't care. I took advantage of those checks.

Lesson #4 — Our Toughest Hardships Are Our Greatest Gifts

I still ask myself, "Why would a father do this to his son?" I wish I had an answer. But I've come to understand that it all comes down to what we're taught. Intentionally or not, each generation passes things down.

My dad was raised in a strict religious background and was given a set of beliefs and expectations that shaped how he saw the world ... and how he saw me. I have no doubt that in his hardline religious views, having a child with my mom put him in a difficult position. Maybe he didn't know how to handle it. And to this day? I believe a part of him still carries that mindset and do believe he has learned to change as well.

Turning Pain into Power

Through this pain, I've learned that it's crucial to validate it, acknowledge it, accept that it's part of me, and to put my stamp of approval on it.

Yes, approval.

Not approval of the behavior. Not the approval of the people who caused it. But approval of the fact that this pain was necessary in order to mold me into a beast of a person. Because my greatest pain is also my greatest gift. Every hardship, every tough moment, every time I questioned who I was and why I was here were the moments that built me. That's where my Empire State of Mind came from, not just from my upbringing, but from every disastrous life event that tried to break me.

Through all of it, I've realized that the toughest hardships are actually gifts. They are lessons. They are fuel. And I have a choice. I can let them push me into the same generational patterns that kept my mother in survival mode, or I can use them to break the chain and build a life where pain isn't a daily chore. I can choose a different path.

The bottom line is this: it's all a choice.

Refusing to Let the Past Define Me

I didn't choose the actions of my parents. In many ways, though, I lived with the consequences.

They showed up in my personality, my emotions, my mannerisms, and in the very spirit that was shaped by how I was raised and treated. But as time has passed, I've learned how to use it for my benefit and will continue to do so. Because at the end of the day, it's in our power to refuse to live life haunted by our past. It's up to us to refuse to let what others did or said dictate the path to our dreams of a better life, dreams of a stable family, dreams of a career that actually brings us joy.

I found my path through basketball. But looking back, I wish I had found something else, too. Basketball was everything to me, but in the long run, it couldn't be the only thing. Because as much as the game saved me, it wrecked me in many moments. You need more than one thing to bring you joy.

At the time, in the environment I was in, I didn't have many options. Knowing what I know now, I make sure to teach that to others.

When I coach the game, when I speak about mental toughness, I remind people: One thing doesn't define you. You have to build multiple avenues for joy, purpose, and growth.

Navigating Difficult Circumstances

You will face times in life when you are placed in difficult circumstances. For me, every time I stepped out of my apartment building, I knew I was walking into something unpredictable.

Lesson #4 — Our Toughest Hardships Are Our Greatest Gifts

When I was young, I had to navigate situations on the fly. From one street corner to the next, something was always happening. Something that could pull you in if you let it. Many of them were not of my choosing

It takes a certain kind of mental toughness that forces you to dig deep into your soul to find the good and to fight off the evil that tries to convince you it's okay.

That inner combat/daily war between right and wrong, between who you are and what the world tries to make you, takes a toll. It wears on your mind. It wears on your body. It wears on your spirit.

The battle isn't just in poverty-stricken areas like the one I grew up in. You can find it anywhere.

In suburban America, kids wake up to a different kind of pressure. They go to school with the weight of expectation pressing down on them. They feel forced to play a role, to meet the standards their families set, to maintain a certain reputation, to protect the prestige their parents care so much about.

But the truth is that kids don't care about that, not in the way their parents do.

The Weight of Manipulation

There are plenty of parents out there that are obsessed with reputation. They create an unspoken rule that their children must uphold a certain status. The pressure they put on their kids to not damage the hierarchy their family has built. And that's also a mentally exhausting environment. Money doesn't remove the pressure. Entitlement doesn't eliminate manipulation. Manipulation exists in every household from the poor to the middle class to the wealthy. It surrounds us all.

The Weight of the Rock

Handling the rock is no easy task, not for a developing teenager, nor for an adult. Every day we're put in situations where we have to choose between the hard and the easy. For me, the hard way was basketball. For you, I hope it's something you love, something that builds you up, and doesn't break you down.

The easy way is where a lot of people fall. I'd be lying if I said I always chose the hard way. There was a time when the pressures at home and the weight of my reality became too much, so I turned to marijuana and alcohol to numb the pain.

Maybe you have, too. And if you have, I don't fault you. At a young age, it's so easy to fall into the trap.

You want acceptance. You want to feel something. You want to be loved.

And when home feels empty, when you feel invisible, sometimes the only place you find that feeling is in the wrong crowd. It makes you feel wanted and seen.

But it also forces another choice ... to stay buried or to climb out. You and I both had a decision: Find a way out or stay buried in the chaos, drowning in substance abuse, trying to escape a pain that won't disappear.

Here's the truth: We all know that using substances to change our bodies and minds, to take the pain away, to take the guilt away, and to disconnect from our reality, isn't good for us.

But at the moment? It works. It takes the pain away. It silences the guilt. It erases the problems, but only for a moment. It lets us step into a different world, where our senses don't have to fight the war we're battling between our ears.

Lesson #4 — Our Toughest Hardships Are Our Greatest Gifts

But after those bad choices, when the high fades, after the buzz wears off, and when reality comes crashing back down, we do learn something. That these unsmart decisions help us learn what our gifts are because these decisions show us exactly who we don't want to be.

The Gift in the Bad Choices

Looking back, my decision to use substances was a bad choice, but it was also a gift. It taught me something real about growing up in that kind of environment. I had plenty of chances to mess up. And with every mistake, I gained a clearer perspective on what I needed to do to put myself on a better path.

I didn't take the path of least resistance; I took the path I was given.

Would I have rather learned those lessons without turning to drugs and alcohol? Of course. But the truth is, my environment and upbringing didn't give me that option. Not at first. I wasn't handed the blueprint to living with kindness and love. I wasn't raised in a place where you naturally saw good deed after good deed, where people modeled what a healthy, positive life looked like. Instead, I was dealt a different hand. The life of drugs and poverty was what I knew. Just like in poker, I had to play the hand I was given and make the best winning hand I could. The hand given if I didn't decide to change could have led me to places some of my closest friends did not escape. It's tranquilizing to think about. One of my closest friends who I call family and my cousin died due to a drug overdose at the age of 41. Another close friend was left paralyzed when a fight ensued that led to him being tossed off the top of an apartment building into scaffolding of another building while on drugs. A high school teammate was shot and killed over a smile at a club while drinking. One of my closest teammates in high school was beaten into a coma by a group of men. Luckily, he survived. A few days after he woke up, he called me. I could barely understand the words projecting over the phone as his speech was lost due to the coma. Over the phone he let me know that his last memory before he woke, was playing basketball with me. This hand was what I wanted to avoid.

Let me be clear: I do not condone using anything that alters your body or mind. But at the same time, I won't deny that my choices (both the good and the bad) helped shape me. Without bad choices, you can't fully understand the value of good ones.

Wherever you are in life, you should see it the same way. No matter where you live, no matter what you've been through, your environment holds lessons that need to be carried forward to your family, your friends, your colleagues, and especially to those you lead so they don't have to make the same mistakes.

Let me be clear one more time. I'm not saying you have to go out and do bad just to learn a lesson. But you can choose to make better choices.

Becoming a Mental Giant

You have to look at the hardships you face as a gift worth sharing. Not to make yourself look good, but because your struggles are priceless and someone can learn from them. Your hardships are worth more than you can imagine because your joy comes from them.

When you push through life's toughest trials, you not only survive, you become a giant and giants are hard to bring down. Giants have the strength to carry heavy burdens, to tear obstacles from the ground and use them as weapons against the very things that try to destroy them.

As a mental giant, your greatest disasters become what fuels you. You don't carry that weight like it's crushing you; you carry it like it's a feather.

Lesson #4 — Our Toughest Hardships Are Our Greatest Gifts

When you become a mental giant, the hardest trials don't break you, they build fearlessness. This fearlessness allows you to face pain, embrace struggle, and handle it all with grace and ease.

The hardship and memory will not completely go away, but here's what you can do to turn your scars into your power:

- You can embrace the scars
- You can then heal from them
- And then you can wear them like a medal of honor

Some scars may be physical and some may be invisible. These scars are proof of what you've endured. They're a reward, something you can take pride in, because they helped you build a fortress of self-belief.

And with that mindset, you don't just survive anymore. You become the hunter, not the hunted. You stop running from life's challenges. You start chasing after what's yours. Nothing stands in your way.

You turn the hard moments into fuel and keep running toward your dream. Mental giants don't starve; they always find a way to feed the fire of hunger inside them.

This is the mental giant you are all capable of becoming.

No Excuses; No Limits

We can't become giants if we let our bad choices, bad upbringings, or bad influences define who we are. We can't become mental giants if we allow our struggles to turn into excuses and complaints.

You made the choice and now you have to own it, learn from it, accept it, carry it, and use it for good.

One of my favorite coaches, John Wooden, once said: "Never make excuses. Your friends don't need them, and your foes won't believe them." What a truth bomb.

At the end of the day, no one really cares about your excuses. So why waste your breath making them?

I get it. It's not easy. We make excuses because we don't want to be judged. We make excuses because admitting fault is uncomfortable. We make excuses because it feels like the easiest way out.

But making excuses actually causes more harm than good. When you put an excuse in your path, you create an obstacle that doesn't need to be there.

You might say, "Well, people just don't understand."

And yeah, some people won't. But guess what? Some people will. And once that moment passes, what's next? This is where you have to take a hard look at yourself. You have to decide if you want to get better, stay stuck or keep falling.

It's a simple choice, but I won't lie to you … depending on the circumstances, it can be complicated as hell.

I share my stories in this book because I want you to know that you are not alone. You're not the first person to struggle with choices, and you won't be the last. You're not the first person who makes excuses, and you definitely won't be the last.

But here's what I've learned: Our choices may seem small at the moment, but over time they become bigger than we ever imagined. Because when you don't own your stuff, when you keep dodging responsibility, it snowballs into something you never saw coming.

And many people think, "Well, this only affects me." But it doesn't. It damages you. It damages the people around you. It holds everyone back.

Lesson #4 — Our Toughest Hardships Are Our Greatest Gifts

That's a reality you don't want to wake up to.

Turning Every Choice into a Gift

Every choice we make comes with pros and cons. That's why I'm telling you to own every choice you make. Whether good or bad, turn it into your greatest gift and never shy away from it.

Your biggest downfalls, your toughest tribulations, and your hardest trials are the greatest things that have ever happened to you. Because they are what shaped you into who you are.

They force growth. They reveal strength you never knew you had. They pull out the best version of you. This is a must to become your greatest self. This is a must to truly understand your worth.

The hardest moments in life are designed to bring out your greatest attributes. They are there to refine you, not break you. Because when you allow adversity to change you, when you lean into the struggle instead of running from it, you grow in ways you never imagined.

And that growth doesn't just make you stronger in one area. You become better at everything.

You'll see transformation in many areas of your life include:

- **Social life**—because you'll stop wasting energy on the wrong people.
- **Emotional life**—because you'll learn how to process pain instead of letting it consume you.
- **Spiritual life**—because you'll start searching for something deeper than the surface-level distractions.
- **Mental life**—because your mind controls it all.

And when your mind is solid and you develop that Empire State of Mind, everything else follows.

Hardships Push Us to Grow

Why is it that the hardest, most unfortunate moments in life are also the ones that give us the greatest opportunities for growth?

I believe it's because there are parts of us we haven't discovered yet. There are pieces of who we truly are that can only be found through struggle.

I never truly reflected on my upbringing, never fully understood the lessons hidden in my struggles, until I lost almost everything I had built as a father, a coach, and a teacher. That's why I wrote this book. That's the reason these mental toughness lessons exist. For the first 20 years of my life, I never realized that my daily battles with poverty and survival were teaching me something. I didn't see that handling the rock (both on the court and in life) was something I was unconsciously doing every single day.

As a kid, I didn't know how to be fully present in my life. And yet, at the same time, I was always in the present because that's where kids live. Most kids are naturally present. That's why they're full of personality, creativity, and fun. They don't overthink. They don't dwell on the past. They're just there, at that moment.

As children, our minds are built on curiosity. We don't have real worries yet, at least not in the way adults do. Some kids are forced to grow up fast. There are children in the world right now dodging bombs and bullets. It's horrific to see on the news, to witness the reality of their daily lives. But for most kids in America, life is still filled with school, play, learning, and exploration. Play is a natural part of childhood. Even in tough circumstances, the stress of life is different as a child.

Lesson #4 — Our Toughest Hardships Are Our Greatest Gifts

We forgive faster. We move on quickly. We investigate life with fresh eyes. But then, somewhere along the way, we stop living in the present. We start worrying more about the future. And you'd think that with all the lessons we learn as kids, we'd carry that ability to be present into adulthood. But we don't. Instead, we're put into boxes. For some of us the key to that box gets thrown away. We become locked away and buried. We forget how to be the creative people we were meant to be.

When life keeps throwing obstacles in your way, when it pulls you off course again and again, it becomes hard to evolve. It took me a long time to rediscover my own creativity. For a while, I thought leaving Brooklyn would help me find it again. But I learned the hard way that the destinations we have planned for our lives never seem to go perfectly or end up exactly how we planned it. For some, it is nothing we ever dreamt of. We think we know where we're headed. But even when we're sure of the path, life has a way of rerouting us. Even when we think we're in control, the truth is, we never really are.

That's the truth for this life, and whatever comes after it. For those of us with a religious perspective, there's one final destination we think of ... Heaven.

The Journey West: A Reality Check

When I stepped out of Brooklyn, I thought I was taking a journey toward a heavenly point on earth, far from the struggles I grew up with. I thought leaving the city would bring clarity, peace, and a fresh start. I never expected life to get even harder.

I left home and headed out west, landing in Rangely, Colorado, out in the middle of nowhere. I was chasing my dream of playing professional basketball. I truly believed that growing up in Brooklyn had prepared me for anything. I thought if I could survive the grit, the grind, and the daily battles of the city, then nothing the world threw at me could compare. I was wrong.

I won't get into the full story of moving out west, but let's just say my plans and expectations didn't exactly match up with reality. What I thought was going to be a clear path toward my future quickly turned into "What the hell just happened?"

It was a journey that tested me in ways I never saw coming. Brooklyn had prepared me for a lot, but not for this.

From Athlete to Educator: An Unexpected Path

The road didn't just stop at playing basketball. When my playing career ended at Southern Utah University, I jumped straight into teaching and coaching. It wasn't something I had planned for; it was something that found me.

Stepping into the education profession brought me into a new kind of battlefield that didn't involve basketballs and scoreboards. Working in classrooms with students, and a whole new level of responsibility, had its own set of trials.

To say it was rocky and challenging is an understatement. It forced me to grow in ways I never expected. And just like basketball, it demanded mental toughness in every sense of the word.

A Crossroads of Life and Death

I want to share a brief story that sums up the reality of my path while living in the West. As a school teacher and coach, I found myself in a precarious position where I had to choose between life and death. I had no training for what was in front of me, no preparation for the weight of the moment.

Lesson #4 — Our Toughest Hardships Are Our Greatest Gifts

As a father with kids who spent half his life helping others, trying to break free from the struggles of my own past, I never imagined I'd be dragged into something that could completely erase two decades of work. Yet, there I was, facing the consequences of someone else's choices.

Lost student. Lost Friend. Struggling parents. Poor Leaders. People I trusted crushed me.

Each of them made a choice that set off a chain reaction, unraveling everything I had built. And this wasn't just about them. It was about the system I was in that created many moments that were harmful. The racism. The harassment. The constant, unspoken battles that I fought followed me throughout my career. It all piled on, brick after brick, until the weight became unbearable.

I never asked for any of it. I never wanted to be forced into this kind of helplessness. But here's the hard truth: Not everything we face in life comes from our own decisions. Sometimes, we get hit with other people's chaos and we have to figure out how to survive it.

A Collision with the Past

All these moments seemed bearable until the last betrayal broke the camel's back. It threw me right back into the same life-or-death battles I had already escaped.

Like I said before, the things we experience as kids never leave us. The trauma, the violence, the pain all sticks with us, buried somewhere deep in our minds until something brings it all rushing back. And in this moment, everything I had tried to lock away came flooding in. But this time it wasn't just the ghosts of my childhood. It was the trauma of my adult life, too.

Empire State of Mind

One of those trauma's was the night I stared death in the face and somehow walked away from the reaper. I survived a drunk driving accident where the driver's sole intent was to kill.

This wasn't a mistake. This wasn't someone who had one too many drinks and made a bad decision. This was intentional. That man got behind the wheel of his car, entered the interstate on the wrong side of the road with his lights off, and barreled forward at full speed fully intending to take out whoever was in his path.

Unfortunately, the first car in his sight was mine.

As my wife and I drove down that dark road, we had no idea death was coming straight for us. I still don't know how we survived. And then, at the last possible second, a voice called my name. It wasn't loud. It wasn't a scream. It was soft. Almost a whisper. But it was loud enough to snap me into awareness.

At that very moment, I saw a flash of light from the reflection of my headlights bouncing off the oncoming vehicle. That was all the time I had. I swerved just in time. Mere feet saved my life. By the grace of God, we escaped.

But my mother-in-law wasn't as lucky. She was driving behind us, trailing my car in her own car with my father-in-law driving his vehicle. And in an instant this drunk driver collided head on. The impact killed her immediately and she was gone.

My father-in-law somehow survived, escaping with just a mild concussion. His car was completely mangled, except for the driver's seat, which was the only part of the vehicle still intact.

And the drunk driver? His SUV was torn in two. You wouldn't believe the wreckage left behind from that night. Twisted metal. Shattered glass. A scene of destruction that looked like something out

Lesson #4 — Our Toughest Hardships Are Our Greatest Gifts

of a movie. That shouldn't have happened. A life taken and a family shattered all because one man decided that his pain, his hopelessness, was enough to put others in the path of destruction. I could call it cowardly but, truthfully, I don't know what that man was going through. I don't know what led him to that moment, to that decision.

But what I do know is that night will never leave me.

When you face death head-on, when you see it up close, when you are the one who finds your loved one lifeless and unrecognizable, it changes you. It marks you.

Scars can heal over time. Scars will always be visible. They are visible to you internally or can be visible externally depending on if the scar is physical. This one? Well, all wounds will always be present once you have the experience.

That's why being mentally sound is everything. Because when life throws something like this at you, when you're left with trauma that can't be undone, you need the mental toughness to endure. Enduring it is a lifetime process and that is something we truly don't comprehend.

Even after facing death and carrying that trauma, it still wasn't enough to prepare me for what came next.

This time, I was fighting a different kind of battle, one that lasted over a year when it came to my livelihood but also became another inner battle of life and death for many including myself. This battle threatened everything I had worked for career wise and my thought of living on this earth as well. I had given my life to education. My time. My energy. My passion.

And yet, there I was standing in a room with a prosecutor who was trying to take my teaching license away for a decision I didn't even make. Placing me in a place that may not give me a chance to take care of my children. This was truly a gut wrenching and mind bending experience I was not prepared for.

The Weight of False Accusations

I had to relive a treacherous situation, one that had the power to ruin my name, to drag my life through the mud, to turn me into a public spectacle for all the wrong reasons. The thought alone sent my mind into chaos. I was fighting for my livelihood, for my family, and fighting against the evil of people who wanted nothing but harm to come my way. And for what? For their own mistakes, their own reckless decisions that ended up hurting others but somehow landed me in the crosshairs.

Every single day, for a year and a half, I woke up feeling like I was walking on thin ice. I had no idea what the next day would bring.

Would I still have a job?

Would I be able to provide for my kids?

Would I lose everything I had built?

And then there was my marriage. Divorce was a real possibility. Everything around me felt like it was either crumbling or had already collapsed. And through it all no one came to my rescue.

Not one school leader stood up for me. Not one parent, who knew my true character, spoke on my behalf. It was just me and my kids trying to grind through life—trying to survive.

Finding Light in the Storm

I found myself seeking help, trying to navigate a life-altering experience that tested me in ways I never imagined. Nothing in my life had ever been easy, and here I was again learning how to handle the rock, but this time as a grown man, facing a trial that felt unbearable.

Lesson #4 — Our Toughest Hardships Are Our Greatest Gifts

This wasn't something an ordinary person could just brush off. It was the kind of battle that breaks people. I was frail. But somehow, I was sturdy enough to keep going. To this day, I don't fully remember how I made it through. I can't recall every detail of what I did each day to survive. But I do know this ... therapy saved me.

It was a price worth paying to keep my mind from drowning in the chaos. It helped me organize my thoughts, helped me process my pain and, most importantly, it helped me turn my trials into something greater. This experience taught me that self-help books are good, and meditation is powerful, but true healing requires more than just reading words on a page or sitting in silence.

Writing became my therapy. It helped me cope and heal some, but it could never erase the scars. The trial that nearly broke me was also the one that turned me into a writer. That's why you're reading these words right now. Because the battle transformed me. It showed me that an Empire State of Mind isn't just about surviving; it's about taking action. It's about doing the hard things that other people call crazy. Like going to therapy, even when people judge you for it. Like choosing to fight back, not with anger, but with purpose.

In basketball, sometimes your greatest defense is your greatest offense and vice versa. And in life the same applies.

When I was defensive, constantly fighting back against the world, my mind was deteriorating. My thoughts weren't wholesome. The hatred and anger I felt toward the people who had wronged me was immeasurable. This trial made me feel every emotion a person can possibly feel.

But the moment I stopped playing defense, I became offensive-minded and took control, and everything started to change.

I made a choice. I refused to live in pain. I refused to let the situation define me. Instead, I used it. I shifted my mindset from victim to creator.

I started to reinvent myself. I unlocked things inside me that I never knew existed like being an author, a writer, and a speaker.

I found a new path in mentoring youth, in helping teachers, in transforming lives through words. But let me be real. Coaching during this time was an extreme burden. I was still finding ways to coach after being let go from this situation I speak of. My kids play the game and are great at it. I joined the club world of basketball so I can still fulfill the joy I had of coaching and coaching my kids. It was very difficult as my reputation in the game for what I do with programs and kids is highly spoken of. My success spoke for itself. This situation caused a lot of people to doubt who I was and left many to speculate including friends due to many rumors and false accusations. I felt the negative energy. Every time I stepped onto the basketball court, I felt the weight. The constant thoughts of what others had heard about me, what they were saying in the community, in the world of my career, in my church, and in my neighborhood was like holding an anvil over my head. A ton of pressure, crushing me from all directions.

But now I know that pressure was reshaping me. It forced me to realize that I had the power to impact more people than I ever imagined. Not just through basketball. Not just through teaching. But through writing. Through speaking. Through helping others handle their own storms.

Finding Light in the Storm

At first, this trial and every trial before it made me feel lost. I kept waiting for the storm to pass. Waiting for the light to return. Waiting for things to get better. Until I realized something huge. You can't just wait for the storm to end. Because you don't know when it will. And if you're just standing there, waiting for a break in the clouds, you're wasting time.

Lesson #4 — Our Toughest Hardships Are Our Greatest Gifts

Instead of waiting for the light outside the storm, I learned to use the little light that exists within it. I stopped looking for the sun, and I started chasing the lightning. Because even in the darkest storms, there is always a spark, a flash of light. And if you can learn to see it, to use it, to let it guide you, you will come out stronger than you ever imagined. There is also an analogy I like to use. It refers to the Bison or Buffalo. When a storm is heading in the direction of a herd of Bison, instead of waiting the storm out, they actually head straight for it. Walking through the storm is easier than waiting it out. This was what I was learning in this dire moment. If you let a storm pick up its pace, it will reach its maximum amount of energy to crush you. So why wait it out. Handle the storm by embracing it not by running from it.

Without these trials pushing me, without finding a way to navigate through them, I wouldn't be the person I am today. I wouldn't be the humble, empathetic, and transformational leader I am becoming. I wouldn't have this Empire State of Mind. I wouldn't be handling the rock the way I do now. This is mental toughness. This is the game. And now I'm built for it.

Forged Through Fire

I needed to become a different man. I will never truly know why all these trials I faced, all the hardships I endured, happened to me. I don't know why life deals some people a cruel hand to fight battle after battle, or why others walk through life seemingly untouched.

But what I do know is that I control my next move. I decide the next direction I will take. And in that choice, I found something new … the birth of a writer.

Was this what I was meant to be all along? I can't say. I don't have that answer. I thought I was meant to be a professional athlete. But I wasn't.

Empire State of Mind

I thought I was destined to be a legendary high school coach, one whose journey would lead to college coaching success. But that was derailed in the blink of an eye. I was rising in the coaching ranks, had even been offered a college job, and just like that it was gone, as fast as flipping off the headlights on your car.

At the end of the day, does it even matter what I do for a living? I don't know.

I built a career in education, but do I love it as much as I used to? No. I fell in love with other things.

Do I still love coaching? Yes. I still get to serve kids and help them grow. I have my own club now. My own kids are thriving in the sport. Their futures are bright.

And even though my path didn't go the way I planned, I know one thing for sure, I have been forged into something stronger. A piece of iron, hammered, heated by the fire to be reinforced, so I can teach others what they are capable of. I'm an iron that sharpens others iron as they say.

I wish I could say, "Please, no more pain. I've had enough." I've already had my fill of trials for a lifetime.

But I know the trials don't stop, not until we take our last breath. Your mind will always be in its own battle. Your body will always face new struggles. Society will always create obstacles in your path. There is opposition in all things. You can't have joy without pain. You can't have peace without suffering.

Handling the rock means understanding this truth. You can't find, develop, or use your purpose without experiencing hardship. When life puts you in a 'tap out' situation, it's not the mistake that defines you. It's not failure or pain. It's your Response. That's what shapes you. That's

Lesson #4 — Our Toughest Hardships Are Our Greatest Gifts

what develops an Empire State of Mind. That's what teaches you how to handle the rock when it's in your hands.

Turning Defense into Offense

In the game of basketball, you play both sides of the ball every possession. You don't get to pick and choose; you have to be solid on both ends. Sometimes, your best offense is your best defense, and other times, your best defense creates your best offense. But then there are days when it feels like you're playing defense the entire game, constantly getting chopped up by the offense, watching them get whatever they want. No matter what you do, nothing seems to go your way. It's frustrating as an individual, and it's even more demoralizing as a team.

At some point, you have to make a choice. You have to look at yourself, look at your team, and say, "Enough. I can't allow this to keep happening." Because if you don't, the results will never change. If you accept it, you'll have no energy left to improve. Your confidence will drain. Your desire to keep fighting will shrink. You'll start believing the lie that bad things will always happen to you. And that feeling of constantly being on the losing end is one of the worst places to be. I've been there, and I know you have too.

Nobody wants to feel like they're getting run over, like they have no control. You build no confidence living in that space. No enthusiasm for what you're doing. No belief in yourself. But here's the thing, if I want to stop the other team from scoring, I have to bear down and guard. If you want to win in life, you have to lock in on both sides of the ball so to speak and go to work. It's that simple. If I want to be unstoppable on offense, I have to work on my craft so that no defense can stop me. I have to put in the reps so that my confidence is unshakable. If I want to be a great defender, I have to improve my stance, my footwork, and my communication with my teammates so that fewer mistakes happen.

I have to be in elite physical shape so that I can keep competing at the highest level and never get tired.

You can't just say you're going to be better. You have to physically show it. You have to get in the gym. You have to make adjustments. You have to study what went wrong and fix it. And when you commit to that, everything starts to shift. The defense improves, which leads to better offensive opportunities. The work starts paying off, and suddenly, the game becomes easier. This isn't just basketball; this is life.

The hardest trials in life give you opportunities, which turn bad defensive possessions in life into fast-break scoring chances that make life more enjoyable. This is what mentally tough people do over and over again. An Empire State of Mind means knowing how to flip the game in your favor. It means turning a losing streak into a championship run. It means turning your setbacks into setups for something bigger.

This applies to everything from your career, your relationships, your business, to your passions. The faster you learn to turn defense into offense, the less time you waste, and the more success follows. Defense in life means surrounding yourself with the right people. It means protecting your vision from those who don't align with it. Offense is knocking on doors, making the calls, showing up rejection after rejection, and still pushing forward until you get the win.

This is how you handle the rock. This is how you play the game. And this is how you take control of your life.

Forged in Fire

The scars left by my greatest trials have given me wisdom to recognize my options, understand how they work, and know how to use them to my advantage. Every hardship, every setback, every painful experience has shaped me. And I've come to see that we are like steel.

Lesson #4 — Our Toughest Hardships Are Our Greatest Gifts

You see, steel on its own is strong, but when exposed to fire, something powerful happens. The intense heat doesn't destroy it. It makes it malleable, adaptable, able to be reshaped into something even stronger. The fire allows the steel to bend, to be transformed. And just like steel, when life puts us through fire, we don't break, unless we allow it.

Only under extreme force does steel actually shatter. And even then, it can be welded back together just like you and me.

This is what mental toughness is all about. This is why the greatest trials in our lives shape us for a lifetime. The more fire we face, the more we learn to withstand it. We grow stronger, not weaker. We develop a level of resilience that makes future challenges less overwhelming. That doesn't mean the pain disappears. It never feels easy at the moment, but mentally we become beasts. We adapt. We evolve.

As our mental strength solidifies, our response to adversity becomes quicker, sharper, more refined. Instead of dwelling on obstacles, we face them head-on. Instead of letting hardships consume us, we use them to fuel us. That's the power of developing an Empire State of Mind.

But here's something else to remember … you don't get through trials alone.

There are always people along the way who help. People who show up in the hardest moments. Never forget that. Mental toughness isn't about going through life as a lone wolf. It's about doing the work yourself but also recognizing the importance of those who support you along the way.

Because in the end, the fire that reshapes us doesn't just come from struggle; it also comes from those who help us rise from it.

The Power of a Support System

The darts of adversity aren't always just internal. Often, the people closest to us can see the struggle before we even acknowledge it ourselves. They notice the exhaustion in our eyes, the weight we carry, the way our energy shifts. And when they do, we can't be afraid to lean on them.

A strong support system is a lifeline. It might come in the form of friends, family, mentors, or even a stranger who shows up at the right moment. I don't believe these encounters are random. There's something spiritual about the way people enter our lives just when we need them most. Our spirits recognize each other, even if we don't fully understand it at the moment. It's an unspoken connection, a silent understanding between two people who may have walked different roads but somehow feel the same struggle.

When you find yourself in those moments when someone reaches out, when a conversation opens up, when you feel that pull to share what's weighing on you, don't hold back. That's where mental strength is built and where healing begins.

Struggles weren't meant to be carried alone. When life gets heavy, these are the people who will remind you of who you are, who will help you clear the fog so you can see the next step. They won't give you the answer, but they'll help you find the intuition to make the right choice.

You won't always take the advice given to you. Sometimes, what they say won't be what you need, but that doesn't mean it wasn't valuable. Even bad advice can be a tool. Sometimes, hearing the wrong suggestion makes you realize exactly what you don't want.

At the end of the day, the choice is yours. You'll feel it when it's right. But never overlook the people who help you get to that point.

Because sometimes their presence alone is what gives you the strength to keep moving forward.

A Brother's Lifeline

Going through that situation as a teacher left me in a dark and lonely place. I was carrying the weight of feeling like I had failed myself, my kids, and my family. Out of all my siblings, I was the only one who escaped the hood, the only one who built a stable life, and here I was, watching it all slip away.

I had everything I dreamed of as a kid: a big house, a nice-sized yard, even the white picket fence I only ever saw on TV. And now it was about to go up in flames.

For months, I kept my pain silent. I didn't want anyone, even my mother, to know. I was stressed, losing weight, and losing my grip on reality. I thought I had built a foundation of toughness through all the things I went through growing up, but this was something different. As a man, I had convinced myself I could handle anything. I grew up in Brooklyn; I could take anything life threw at me. But that proved to be a lie. I couldn't handle it, and I was losing myself mentally.

I needed a hand to pull me through the despair, but I didn't know where to turn. Therapy helped, but there's something about having a personal connection with someone who truly knows you that makes all the difference. I had spoken to friends and family, but I couldn't bring myself to spill my darkest truth. I was ashamed. I felt like a failure. Even though none of it was my fault, I couldn't shake the feeling that I had let everyone down.

Then, one day I got a phone call. It was from Prentice, my big bro, the same man I spoke about earlier in this book. Every now and then, he would call just to check in on me, to see how I was doing. He had always been there for me, not just as a basketball mentor, but as a big brother in life.

That day, when he called, I almost lied. He asked how coaching was going, and I told him, "All is well." I tried to keep up the front, told him I was still grinding, still working to take my team to the next level. I wanted him to believe I had everything under control.

But I couldn't hold it in. I broke. "P," I said, my voice shaking, "I might lose everything, big bro."

There was a pause. Then, he asked me what I meant. "P," I said, fighting back tears, "I might lose my coaching job, my teaching job, and I'm in a family crisis right now. I don't even know if my family is going to stay together."

Prentice listened. He let me spill all the details, the frustration, the helplessness. I told him how I felt trapped, how I couldn't believe that after all the hard work I put in, I was about to lose it all.

I told him, "I feel like I let everyone down." After I got it all out, he didn't hesitate.

"Little bro," he said, "I'm proud of you."

I froze.

"I'm so happy to call you my little brother," he continued. "What you just told me makes me want to love you even more."

I couldn't even respond.

Then he asked, "How are the kids doing?"

"They're okay," I said.

"Good. Do they know you still love them?"

"Yeah."

Lesson #4 — Our Toughest Hardships Are Our Greatest Gifts

"That's what matters." Then he asked about my wife.

"It's a struggle," I admitted.

"Fight through it," he told me.

"I'm trying my best," I said.

"I know you are."

Then, he hit me with words that changed everything for me. "Little bro, you are not a disappointment. You are not a failure. And you sure as hell aren't what people are saying or thinking about you right now.

"You've accomplished a lot, and people became jealous. People felt slighted. They hated your success and that isn't your fault. You treated people right. You did things the right way. That's why you accomplished so much, so quickly. That's why this is happening. And I need you to know that you are strong enough to handle it. There is no doubt in my mind."

Then, he said something that nearly broke me.

"You know I got you. I will always be here for you. I don't care how far apart we are. It is my duty to check up on you. That's my promise. And I will keep it."

We talked for a little longer, and then we hung up.

That conversation changed me. And Prentice kept his word. Since that day, he has called or texted me every single Thursday. We call it Family Thursday. Every Thursday morning, I wake up and see a message from my big bro. Every week without fail. We are two hours apart due to distance in time zone but his text at 8am my time and 6am his, always pops up.

"Good morning, little bro. How's the family? How are you holding up?"

"Happy Family Day."

It's been years now, and he's never missed a single one. Not even my mother or father or siblings check in on me like that.

That's not a knock on them, but for a man with no blood relation to me, who has different colored skin, different religious views, and a completely different background to be the one who checks in on me every single week without fail is something special. That's real love. That's a real family.

And now, every Thursday I wake up looking forward to that text. What a blessing it is to have a brother like that.

The Gift Hidden in the Trial

The gauntlet of life has put me through more pain than I could have imagined, but through it all, my greatest trial brought me my greatest connection. The deep, meaningful relationships I had built when I was younger that shaped me as a kid came back 20 years later to lift me up when I was at my lowest. I was practically rotting away, feeling like a discarded, bruised piece of fruit, and my brother helped me off the ground.

So my question to you is this: Who is in your corner?

Who will be there when life knocks you down?

Who will stand by your side not just in the good times, but when you're at rock bottom?

Because when you're going through the hardest moments of your life, that's when you find out who's really in your corner. That's when you see who's willing to go through the fire with you.

For me, my greatest trial brought the greatest gifts in the form of people. Just like Prentice reached out and reminded me of who I was and Mike Senior, the man I dedicated this book to, did the same.

During a visit back to Brooklyn, I had to sit down and tell Mike the full story. I explained everything, the pain, the struggle, the weight of it all. And when I did, his response was exactly what I needed. He didn't judge me. He didn't place blame. He didn't dwell on what went wrong. He embraced me with love. Mike made sure I knew who I was and who I needed to be.

His words, like Prentice's, held me up when I didn't have the strength to stand on my own.

The Power of Vulnerability

Never be afraid to share your hurt with others. You never know what they've been through, what wisdom they might offer, or how your struggle might be the inspiration they need to push through their own battles.

We tend to keep our pain locked away, afraid that opening up makes us look weak. But the truth is, real strength is found in vulnerability. My willingness to share allowed me to develop impenetrable bonds with men who had always seen the good in me, even when I couldn't see it myself. Not once did they judge me. Not once did they place blame. All they did was encourage, uplift, and remind me that I still had work to do.

Restoring Faith in Trust

For most of my life, I've had trust issues. I didn't trust people. I didn't trust their intentions. I didn't trust that anyone would be there for me when I really needed them. But this experience gave me hope that real relationships exist, that there are people who will stand by you even when you feel completely alone. Even though these men were far from me physically, they were right next to me spiritually.

They spoke the words I needed to hear. They gave me back the perspective I had lost. They reminded me that I wasn't alone.

And in that moment, I realized my greatest trial wasn't just about me. It was about strengthening my relationships. It was about building trust. It was about learning that I wasn't meant to carry the weight alone. The trial, as painful as it was, ended up being one of my greatest blessings.

The outpouring of love from Prentice and Mike was a major part of my healing. Their words and their presence (even from a distance) helped pull me back from the edge. They reminded me of my strength, my worth, and my purpose.

But what I didn't know at the time was that another life-changing event was about to happen. Something that would catapult me back toward positivity, back toward optimism, back toward truly wanting to live.

At my lowest I wasn't sure life was worth living. I had reached a breaking point. The weight of the pain, the betrayal, the feeling of having my entire life crumble before my eyes had me spiraling out of control. The thoughts of ending it all crept in. I didn't see a way forward.

For so much of my life, the people who were supposed to love me were thousands of miles away—both figuratively and literally. They weren't standing right next to me. It makes you feel so alone. And when you feel that aloneness, when the people closest to you have hurt you the most, it's an isolation that's hard to explain. It's numbing.

I had spent my life giving back. As a teacher and coach, I dedicated myself to helping young people. As a husband and father, I gave everything to my family. I poured love into others, yet somehow, in my darkest moments, I felt empty. But here's what I learned. Sometimes,

Lesson #4 — Our Toughest Hardships Are Our Greatest Gifts

when you feel like you have nothing left, your biggest blessings come from the places you least expect. The people outside your immediate circle that you didn't even realize were watching end up being the ones who lift you up in ways you never saw coming. And this is a lesson I will never forget.

An Unexpected Blessing

Sometimes, the smallest message can change everything.

I was scrolling mindlessly through Facebook, wasting time, drowning in my own misery, feeling like my life was slipping through my fingers. Social media was an escape, but not a good one. It was a place to sulk, to compare, to wish for a life that wasn't mine. I was caught in the trap so many of us fall into scrolling through highlight reels, watching everyone else's happiness, and wondering why I couldn't feel the same. I wasn't looking for anything. I was just trying to take my mind off my reality.

Then, out of nowhere, I got a message. It was from Manny Teolii, a former player of mine. We had stayed in touch here and there, but I didn't expect to hear from him that day.

His message was simple: "Hey coach, how are you doing?"

Reluctantly, I answered. "I'm hanging in there."

He replied quickly. "That's good. I have some great news and wanted to let you know."

I paused for a second.

Then his next message came through. "My wife is pregnant, and I'm going to be a dad. I'm so excited."

A Name That Changed Everything

I replied quickly back while still processing the message. "Congrats, man! I'm happy for you." Then I asked the natural follow-up question, "Is it a boy or a girl?"

Manny responded, "It's a boy."

I smiled at my phone and responded, "Man, I'm jealous. I always wanted a boy, but I'm lucky to have four girls."

Then Manny hit me with something I wasn't expecting. "Hey coach, what do you think I'm going to name him?"

I paused for a second. Why would he ask me that? I figured we had a lot in common, so maybe he was naming his son after something we both loved. We both collected Jordan sneakers, so I threw out a guess. "Is it Jordan?"

"No."

Okay, maybe something else we bonded over—the New York Jets. "Is it Jet?"

"No."

Now I was stumped. "Alright, man, I give up. What's his name going to be?"

Then I saw it. A single message. "Coach, I'm naming my son Khalil. After you."

I froze. Stunned. It was like something out of a movie. I couldn't believe what I was reading. I sat there, staring at my screen, unable to move. Then, without warning, tears started streaming down my face. Never in my life had I imagined something like this. Never had I thought a former player of mine would name their child after me.

Lesson #4 — Our Toughest Hardships Are Our Greatest Gifts

I had to catch my breath. After a moment, I finally typed out a response. "Manny, I can't let you do that. There's no need for this."

His reply came instantly. "No, coach. I know we don't talk much, but you have no idea how big of an impact you made on my life when you coached me. I was doing things I wasn't supposed to back in high school, but you never gave up on me. You never gave up on any of us. You helped change my life around. It's only right that I name my son after a man I look up to."

I didn't know what to say.

Then he added one last thing. "My wife agrees. We both love the name, but it makes it even more meaningful that we get to name him after someone who is a great example to me."

I sat there, completely overwhelmed. In an instant, Manny's words shattered all the pain I had been feeling, all the doubts, all the moments where I questioned my worth.

After that emotional conversation with Manny, I had to reevaluate everything. The path I was heading down wasn't sustainable. I was drowning.

I love my children with all my heart, and I was living for them, trying to push through the PTSD, the depression, and the anxiety that had been eating me alive since my life had spiraled out of control. But the truth was, I wasn't okay.

I was taking sleeping pills. I was taking depression pills. I was having mental breakdowns. And in those moments, I became someone I didn't recognize. The anger that had built up inside me for years exploded, and I would go on tirades, lashing out at the world, putting people down, and, worst of all, scaring my own children.

Empire State of Mind

They didn't know what was happening to their dad. I didn't know what was happening to me. The trauma from everything I had gone through had torn me apart. I had spent years holding it all in, convincing myself that I could handle anything. But in reality? I was breaking.

And then, Manny's message changed everything. This wasn't just a moment of kindness. It wasn't just a compliment or a nice gesture. This was a spiritual gift, a reminder that even in my darkest moments, I had made an impact.

And now? I had another responsibility. One day, this little boy will grow up and ask about his name. And when that day came, I needed to make sure that the name he was given (my name) was one he could be proud of. That when he heard the name Khalil, it would mean something. It would mean strength. It would mean resilience. It would mean love. It would mean "Friend," the true meaning of the name. In Arabic Khalil means friend. This meant I had to keep living. Not just for my kids. Not just for my former players. For myself.

The Gift That Changed Everything

The gift that Manny gave me helped turn my greatest trial into my greatest gift. Since that day, I've tried my best to live differently. To wake up each morning and fight through the darkness. To pull myself out of the abyss of helplessness that I still battle with, because let's be real, some scars never fully fade and will never heal completely. Both physically and mentally they are marks on you that stain you forever.

Manny gave me strength. He reminded me that even when life feels like it's crushing you, faith and integrity still matter. That even when the world tries to tear you down, you can still stand tall. This moment wasn't just life-changing; it was life-saving.

Lesson #4 — Our Toughest Hardships Are Our Greatest Gifts

Manny's message saved my family. At the time, everything around me was on the verge of collapse. I was fighting for my career, my character, my sanity. I was drowning in the pain of being falsely accused, misunderstood, and left to fight a battle that felt unwinnable.

But suddenly, the thing that had felt like my greatest hardship was flipped on its head. Manny had given me a reason to fight. He gave me proof that what I had dedicated my life to mattered. He reminded me that even when the world tries to break you, there are people who will stand up and prove that you made a difference.

And in that moment, I realized: I can't stop now.

As a business owner, speaker, author, and a mentor, I now use this story to inspire students, teachers, and anyone willing to listen. Because when you handle the rock the right way, when you share your gifts with the world, when you lead with integrity, it always comes back to you. Maybe not in the way you expect. Maybe not in the way you planned. Maybe not even in a way you'll ever see. But it matters. Because even the smallest things can change a life.

The Power of a Legacy

One of the greatest lessons I have ever learned is that mental toughness at its finest is in understanding that the little things we do matter most. Especially when it feels like no one is watching. Especially when it seems like your efforts are going unnoticed. Because in the long run? They do matter.

Having my name passed down to another generation is an honor and a huge responsibility. It's a reminder that I have a duty to live up to.

I now have a young boy and a family who see me as a highly favored figure who makes a difference in the world. That's not something I take lightly. It's something I will honor for the rest of my life.

Manny's journey taught him how to give back, just like I tried to do for him. He took the trials he faced, reflected on the lessons I had once given him, and turned them into a gift for his family and for me. And by naming his son after me, he gave me something I can never fully express gratitude for … a reminder that even in our darkest moments, the light we shine for others will always stand true.

Turning Trauma into Transformation

Manny turned my trauma into transformation. That day, I was changed. He gave me strength. He showed me that my pain had a purpose and it wasn't pointless. He showed me that every struggle, every heartbreak, every moment I thought was breaking me was actually building me.

Pain is for progress. Pain is productive if you channel it. Pain is for peace if you learn how to use it.

This is what the greatest hardships are for. They don't just test us; they shape us. They give us opportunities to help others fight through their own battles, just like Manny and "P" did for me.

And the crazy thing? I know they understood my pain before I ever said a word. That's the power of genuine connection. That's what happens when you lead with good. You form relationships with people who can feel your struggle, even when they don't know the details.

And when life feels insurmountable, when you think no one understands, remember that there are people out there who truly care and have been impacted by your presence, your kindness, your actions. And whether you realize it or not, those good deeds you've put into the world will come back to you. Often in ways, and at times, you never expect.

Lesson #4 — Our Toughest Hardships Are Our Greatest Gifts

Fuel for the Journey

"P" and Manny gave me just enough fuel for an empty tank to get my car started again. Without their blessings, their words, their actions, I don't know if I would have been able to start climbing another mountain in my life. I don't know if I would have found the strength to chase another peak after everything had collapsed around me.

Writing this book? I never would have dreamed of it.

I would have never imagined this idea if these men hadn't reminded me of something I thought was ripped from my heart, the ability to believe in something again.

The authenticity and genuine heart I had always carried could have been lost forever. But these men gave me a reason to search for it. To rescue my mind and heart from the darkness that tried to consume them.

The truth is, this suffering had to happen. The anger, the bitterness, the pessimism that infected me had to run its course so that I could learn how to fight through it. This isn't just my story; it's your story, too. You have to allow your greatest hurt to become your greatest gift. That's what it means to have an Empire State of Mind. That's what it means to be mentally strong enough to rise above the shame, the guilt, and every emotion that tries to hold you back.

Handling the rock of your greatest tribulation will be felt before you even say a word. It will show in how you carry yourself. It will show in how you walk into a room. People will notice something different. They'll say, "You've changed."

And your answer will be, "Yes, I have."

Not in who you are, but in how you handle who you are. And once you understand that, you'll start living with purpose again. And nothing beats that feeling. This is the gauntlet of life. The trials will come, no doubt. But when you learn that your greatest gift is hidden inside your greatest trial, your heart and mind will align in a way that allows you to do the unthinkable.

CHAPTER 6

Mental Toughness Lesson #5 – Read the Words from the Greatest Minds

We're living in a time unlike any other in human history. This is a time when information is available at the speed of light. With a simple click on a computer, tablet, or phone, you can access an infinite amount of knowledge. All you have to do is type in what you're looking for, and within seconds, it's right there in front of your eyes. With the rise of artificial intelligence, the game has changed even more. Knowledge can now be generated for you, even without typing a single word. It's an incredible accomplishment for humanity, but in my humble opinion, it can also be dangerous. AI can either be one of mankind's greatest tools or one of its greatest threats, blurring the lines between what's real and what's not.

As I've poured hours into writing this book, some might wonder, "Did AI write this?" Let me be clear—absolutely not. This is all me. All human. AI may be helpful in some ways, but it can't match the intuition, experience, or heart of a real person. It can't replicate what comes from

Lesson #5 – Read the Words from the Greatest Minds

the soul. I want to be original, to truly inspire people through genuine, human connection and through words that come from a real place, not a machine. The truth is, AI has made it hard to tell what's real and what's not. It challenges the reliability of the information we receive. But even with all this tech, I believe we'll always yearn for something much deeper ... authenticity. Real words from real people. And those words? You'll still find them on the shelves of libraries around the world or on Amazon, depending on how you like to read.

Escaping the Scroll: Taking Back Control

You have a choice in this world. You can spend your time endlessly scrolling through Instagram reels, TikTok videos, Twitter (X) threads, or Facebook clips, hooked on an algorithm that feeds your addiction. Before you know it, hours have passed, and you've accomplished nothing, glued to a screen that's convincing you life is just a highlight reel filled with shortcuts to fame and fortune. That's the daily battle we face in this digital age. We are fighting a system designed by savvy minds to keep us distracted while making them wealthy.

But here's the truth: you have a savvy mind, too. You have the power and potential to create the life you want, and you don't need AI or social media to make it happen. Social media can be a great tool to connect with others, but it's not the source of real success. That comes from within.

Do Your Homework: There Are No Shortcuts

The goal is to shift our mindset and start using this infinite resource of knowledge to actually serve the life we're living. There are endless podcasts, online radio shows, and YouTube channels all offering free games to help you chase your dreams. All you have to do is search for the recipe that fits you. Find what resonates, but don't get fooled by something that looks good on the surface but has no substance underneath. I call it doing your homework. Do the research before diving into something that might not be real.

There's no such thing as a shortcut when it comes to knowledge. Real knowledge has to be applied consistently over time before you see the results. Sure, you can hop on YouTube and find someone who claims they've cracked the code on selling or marketing something. You might even try to copy it but somehow it just doesn't land the same. It's like trying to recreate your favorite restaurant meal or your granny's cooking at home. You can follow the steps, but it never tastes exactly like the original. The beauty is, through trial and error, you start creating your own flavor. One that feeds your soul. You adjust the recipe, make it yours, and in that process, you find your path. You can't duplicate someone else's exact formula, but you can learn from it and remix it into something that works for you. And when you get that, you're well on your way.

Knowledge Is Power—Only When Applied

No matter how complex the issue, there's a solution floating somewhere out there in the metaverse just waiting to be discovered. Answers to life's biggest questions like career changes, healing, learning new skills are all accessible if you're willing to look. I'm pretty sure if I wanted to build a plane from scratch, I could find every step online. Piece by piece, video by video, tutorial by tutorial. Eventually, if I followed it all and applied myself, I could get that plane built and fly anywhere I wanted to go.

But let's be real. I'd have to learn how to build it first, and then, most importantly, I'd have to practice. Like Allen Iverson once said in his classic, unforgettable press conference: "Practice? We talkin' about practice?" He might've been able to skip it from time to time, but if

Lesson #5 – Read the Words from the Greatest Minds

I'm trying to be a pilot, that mindset won't fly—literally. I'd need to become both a skilled builder and a trained pilot. And just watching videos or reading step-by-step online wouldn't cut it. You can't just consume knowledge; you've got to apply it, test it, and earn it through repetition. Otherwise, you're heading straight for disaster. Some things require more than just a screen and a search bar. They require time, discipline, and real world experience.

This leads to the question: How does this relate to handling the rock? What does this have to do with an Empire State of Mind? Knowledge is the foundation of growth. True knowledge helps build a successful mind.

The real question becomes: Are you using knowledge to manipulate and take advantage of others, or are you using it to inspire and uplift them?

Mentally tough individuals understand that knowledge is about discernment, humility, and impact, not just facts. They use what they learn not to elevate themselves above others, but to build bridges, share value, and bring people up with them. They know the information they gather is meant to sharpen their tools, not just for self-gain, but to be of service to others.

Mental toughness is owning where you are right now in life, and still committing to growth. It's having the humility to say, "I don't know," and the strength to go figure it out. It's being relentless about improving your craft and refining the traits you were gifted with to become a better version of yourself emotionally, spiritually, mentally, and physically. No matter what's happening in the world around you, the knowledge you pursue and apply is meant to help you show up better in the present. And when you reach a point of confusion or unfamiliarity, the mentally tough don't hide from it, they look for clarity.

Empire State of Mind

Not understanding something isn't a weakness; staying stuck in misunderstanding is. The mind may never know everything, but that's not the point. The point is to keep learning, keep growing, and keep evolving. That is an Empire State of Mind. That is handling the rock.

As much as people want to say, "Hey, come follow me, I have the secret recipe to making you successful," the truth is there are no secrets. The secrets are out of the bag. There are no hidden whispers from the world only shared with a chosen few. Everything you need is already out there. We all have access to it. We all can find the information we need to go where we want to go.

Knowledge is literally floating in the metaverse right now as I speak, waiting to be captured, waiting to be used. But to truly build upon what you currently have as a human being, you must be willing to learn from someone who's either been there already or is currently walking the path you're trying to take. This cycle never stops. You want more. I want more. We all want more. That's part of being a human.

Every single one of us has ideas. There are billions of people on this planet, and someone else is thinking what you're thinking right now. Maybe it's not word for word, but the idea is there. I know as I write this book, someone else is probably writing a book on mental toughness too. There are others who already have. They each have their own version, their own story to tell, just like I do. And like me, they're tired of holding it in. They want to help others avoid the pain they've endured. Just like someone out there is looking for a book like this because they're ready to become mentally tougher. They're searching for insight, tools, and a story that speaks to them.

At the end of the day, we're all trying to get to a finish line starting from the same place. And the best way to get there? Read the words from the greatest minds who've ever walked this earth.

Lesson #5 – Read the Words from the Greatest Minds

Learning From the Greats

Now, are there people out there who might be smarter or more intelligent than those who write books? Absolutely. I'm sure of it. I certainly don't have access to the smartest people on the planet in person. The only way most of us can connect to the greatest minds of the world is through books, podcasts, interviews, speeches, streams, and the many outlets technology provides us. We can't sit in a room with them face-to-face, but we can sit with their thoughts, their perspectives, and their lessons through what they've left behind. That's the power of the written word. That's how knowledge has always been passed on and how it will continue to be passed on.

Reading matters. It always has. Without written records, how would we know how to build the lives we want to live? How would we know how past civilizations survived, grew their people, built incredible cities, created infrastructures that allowed their societies to thrive? It all comes from written history. The wisdom of those who came before us was preserved through writing and those words are how trades, cultures, values, and innovations were passed from generation to generation. That's how people living in poverty became middle class. That's how middle-class people rose to lead nations, or even became kings and queens. The written word told their story. The written word tells the stories of heroes we never met but will never forget.

These aren't secrets locked away for a chosen few. These are lessons and insights written for all of us so we can find our own greatness. Without the written word, none of what we know would exist. Our society, our knowledge, our traditions, even our deepest beliefs wouldn't have survived. None of the wisdom we quote, the history we teach, the lives we admire would have been preserved without the written word. Without it, all of that would've vanished like a breeze in the wind.

Marcus Garvey, a political activist during the 1920s to 1940s who worked to influence politics for Black people in both the U.S. and England, once said, "A people without the knowledge of their past history, origin and culture is like a tree without roots." How true that statement is. It applies to every aspect of our lives. If we don't have knowledge of the past, how can we possibly understand our present, let alone build a better future?

Robert A. Heinlein, a science fiction author, aeronautical engineer, and naval officer is often referred to as the "dean of science fiction writers." Heinlein said, "A generation which ignores history has no past and no future." I agree with him wholeheartedly. How do we know where we're going if we don't know where we came from? These two individuals are remembered because what they did was written down, preserved, and shared. I was able to find their words, learn from them, and now I'm sharing them with you here on these pages. I found knowledge, and I applied it. That's not a secret. That's the formula. That's how the world has become what it is.

Men and women throughout history have passed down written knowledge that helps us grow. Reading comprehension, when truly understood and applied, becomes a powerful piece of your mental toughness. But it only matters if you choose to act on it. You have to take these so-called secrets of our past and use them to shape your dreams, build your life, and help you grow into a better human being.

Celebrities Aren't Superhuman—They're Students Too

Reading the last two paragraphs, you may have never heard of these men. They weren't the wealthiest. They didn't sit on a throne, and they came from humble beginnings. These were men who made an impact in their particular field. They are not billionaires, not leaders of massive

Lesson #5 – Read the Words from the Greatest Minds

armies or world-famous generals. They made history in their own lane. And it just so happens that either they or someone who believed in their story decided to write about their experiences and preserve their words for the generations that would come after them. This is how the cycle works. I'm sure they learned to use what they were taught from those who came before them just like you and I are learning from men like them today.

"I've been completely fascinated with history because it tells everything about what's going to happen next because it's cyclical; everything repeats in general." That quote comes from Emilie Autumn, an American violinist from my generation that I recently came across. And she's absolutely right. History is a continuous cycle of events, shaped by men and women who studied the past to create the future they envisioned. You and I hold that same power in our hands, but we have to be willing to use it.

Now think about the wealthiest and most influential people of our time as I write this—Elon Musk of Tesla, Jeff Bezos of Amazon, Jay-Z the rap mogul, Kim Kardashian the reality TV icon, Kevin Hart the face of comedians today, and Kamala Harris, the first African American and Indian woman to become Vice President of the United States. Do you think they achieved all this through some secret formula no one else has ever had access to? Not at all. Many of them didn't come from privilege or start with a head start in life. What they did do was use the knowledge and lessons passed down from others before them. They learned from those who paved the way, reading the words of great minds, and applying what they learned. Elon Musk didn't even name Tesla after himself; he honored a mind from the past. That's what mental toughness and growth look like. It's not about inventing something from nothing. It's about absorbing knowledge, applying it, and turning it into something meaningful.

Lighting Your Own Fire

I want you to understand something: many people think these successful individuals have all the wisdom, like they're the smartest to ever do it. That's not the case. We cling to their words like they're gold, as if they were handed down from the heavens. Many idolize humans just because they've achieved riches, and they attach themselves to their words because those people live in luxury. But the real luxury isn't the material, it's in the wisdom and in the act of applying it. What these individuals have truly done is take the knowledge and lessons of those who came before them, scale it, and add their own touch and maybe a little sprinkle of luck. At the end of the day, that wisdom didn't originate with them, it was passed down from generations before, often from humble men and women whose names we may never know.

The knowledge we see displayed by celebrities or industry leaders often has roots in the quiet wisdom of everyday people, warriors of life who endured without recognition. Those famous faces we see? They're not the only ones who carry wisdom. They were simply the ones who decided to share it from the spotlight they were given. The truth is, successful people are influenced by ordinary people more than we realize. Society has made it seem like the wealthy and well-known have it all figured out. That's not true. They wrestle with the same mental battles we all face, just in different circumstances. Depression, anxiety, betrayal, sickness, illness don't spare the rich. Sure, money might make some parts of life easier, but pain still shows up at the doorstep. It just wears a different face. Whether you're wealthy or not, the principles behind life's struggles remain the same.

We all need to find wisdom, especially when it comes to dealing with the adversity of life and handling that rock when it comes our way. When it comes to mental toughness and breaking through the barriers in our minds, the words I speak of are valuable but only when

Lesson #5 – Read the Words from the Greatest Minds

we truly internalize them and apply them. There's more to it than just consuming content. As we pick up books from our favorite authors, listen to motivational speakers, scroll through our social feeds, or get fired up by quotes from celebrities or influencers, we often don't realize that this kind of motivation is mostly surface-level. It doesn't last. It doesn't fulfill us completely. And it's not sustainable.

These external motivators might give us a quick spark, but they're not the fire that keeps us going. We have to learn how to turn that extrinsic motivation into something intrinsic that lives inside of us, not just something we rely on from the outside. At some point, all that inspiration has to become a reminder, not a lifeline. What matters is the wisdom we've gathered and embedded in our own minds, so when we face the hard stuff, we don't need to go looking for a quote or video to keep moving. We already have the words we need inside us.

No celebrity was with me on the court when I was grinding. It was just me and my thoughts. No music in my ears, no one clapping for me. Because when the music stops and the lights go out, what are you left with? Just you. Your own thoughts. That's why the motivation from your feed fades fast, and why relying on someone else's fire will never keep you lit. No celebrity whispered in my ear when I was writing this book. No powerful quote made me sit down and type these words. I told myself to get it done. I just worked.

When I sat at my computer and didn't feel like writing, I reminded myself of what I've been through, how far I've come and why I never want to go back. I think about whose life I might help change. What athlete or student might need to read this. Not a single celebrity sparked that thought. It came from my own fire, my own mentors, my own reading, my own good and bad experiences in coaching, education, and in life.

Empire State of Mind

And now, you're reading these words from me. I'm not famous. I'm not a household name. But I'm known by you, and that's what matters. We get so caught up clinging to the words of celebrities, thinking they're the only ones who can inspire us. But there are powerful, life-changing books out there written by people you've never heard of and their words might just shift your world. Because ultimately, it's not about who said it; it's about what you do with it.

You are your own energy source. You get to change your thoughts. You get to create the fire in your own life. Someone else might give you that first spark, but you've got to pour your own gas on your own fire if you want to keep it burning. Once that outside motivation runs out, how do you sustain your flame? The only way is to buy your own gas, keep your own tank full, and drive your own vehicle. That's mental toughness. That's how you handle the rock.

How do you create your own gas? That's the next question we should ask ourselves. And what I'm about to tell you might surprise you. When I was facing the near-total destruction of my basketball and teaching career, everything I thought I had learned, everything I had built my life on, suddenly felt like it vanished. All the hours I had spent developing myself, all the reading, all the studying, all the practice all seemed to disappear the moment I needed it most. It was like none of it mattered anymore. The strength I once had wasn't there. No quote I had memorized, no motivational clip, no philosophy could bring me back to that moment. I was an ordinary man, standing in the middle of a storm, suffocating in my thoughts.

I had invested countless hours on the court, in books, in classrooms, in conversations in order to become one of the best in my field. I had a solid reputation, known for my work ethic and my passion. People in the basketball world knew my name, and not for the wrong reasons. But when this hardship hit, it erased all of that from my mind. It was

Lesson #5 – Read the Words from the Greatest Minds

like someone had pressed delete on my identity. I couldn't breathe, couldn't think clearly, and I couldn't hold onto anything positive. The wisdom I once used to stand tall felt like it was gone. The character I had built brick by brick through discipline and learning had evaporated. I was drained, like a body dehydrated with no fluids left to give. The fluid was my passion. My desire to keep improving through reading, learning, and applying knowledge was gone. I reached for it, but it was out of reach. I was too weak to grab the rope that once pulled me forward.

I felt like I had nothing left. I tried everything. I opened books and revisited the lessons. But nothing gave me what I needed. I searched within, hoping that the resilience I had as a kid, as a young kid from Brooklyn, would rise again. But it didn't, at least not right away. So I had to do something I had always been afraid of. I had to take a step I once thought was for the weak, but I soon learned it was actually for the strong. I had to find my passion for life again and did it through mental therapy.

The Strength to Heal

Many people still believe that if you seek therapy or talk to a therapist you must be crazy. But it's actually the complete opposite. The truth is, therapy is one of the most powerful, life-changing tools we have. The knowledge you gain about yourself through that process can be transformative. With all of the chaos, the heartbreak, the near collapse of everything I built that I had gone through, it made me realize it was time to face it all head-on and handle the rock in a way I had never done before: through healing.

Having an Empire State of Mind means being courageous enough, brave enough, to admit when you need help. It means facing the most difficult person in your life ... yourself. You are your biggest challenge.

You are the one you have to figure out if you want to grow. I was lost because I didn't understand myself. And that's the truth for so many of us. When we take the time to really understand who and what we need, what makes us healthy, and what triggers our pain, we finally start to see through the dark. And when we stop overthinking about the things that hurt us, when we get intentional about our healing, we can begin building a life that feels good again.

Wisdom Begins Within

Some of the greatest words I've ever heard that brought me wisdom, belief in myself, and helped me regain my value and worth came from conversations with my therapist. Yes, my therapist. Not some famous man or woman, but a wise individual who's spent years helping people repair their minds and find reasons to believe life is still worth living. And this person taught me that the only way to truly live is by understanding yourself in a way only you can. You might be thinking, "Is he serious?" I am. Without a doubt. As a coach, educator, teacher, and speaker, I've learned from some of the greatest minds that ever walked this planet through books, quotes on walls, Instagram posts and TikToks filled with valuable life tools. But the truth is, the greatest wisdom comes from your own lived experiences. Those words from others just help activate what's already inside of you.

We pack our minds with so much negative energy that we go searching for someone else's words to remind us of what we've forgotten. We've always been in control of our own minds. Those famous men and women we look up to? Somewhere along the way, they trained their minds to lean into optimism, into purpose. That wasn't an accident. Maybe a bit of DNA, but for most it was learned. That mindset was molded through trials, failure, persistence, and reflection. It was built. And many of them will tell you they didn't start

Lesson #5 – Read the Words from the Greatest Minds

out that way. They struggled too. They were hard on themselves, beat themselves up, doubted everything. They had to battle those same dark thoughts. Author Jon Gordon, known for his work on positivity, says it best: "Don't be an energy vampire." Don't suck the light out of yourself or others. We often think of energy vampires as other people, but in reality, we are our own vampire. We suck the life out of ourselves. Our own voice does the most damage. That inner leech sucking us dry of our own positivity. Before we can silence the negativity around us, we've got to confront the energy vampire within. That's where it starts.

No one wants to live in darkness, even those who are in it. There's a light unseen but deeply felt that we all crave in our lives. And when we can't find it within ourselves, we often look to others to help us locate it.

My therapist reminded me over and over: it's *you* who needs to find *you*. That's where it starts. I had to learn how to truly listen again, not just hear. To read again without skimming, but to deeply absorb what I was reading. I found my way back to books that once filled my mind with fire: self-help books, coaching books, speaking books. These became the ammunition I needed to kill the darkness growing inside me. Because when you're in a dark place, you start desperately searching for answers, reaching outward for insight, hoping that something will help you turn inward and unlock what's always been inside of you.

That's the elusive power of light. It hides at times. But with the right people, the right words, and the right actions, you can chase it down and harness it, even when it feels impossible. Knowing your purpose re-ignites something inside you. And the truth is, we all hunger for it daily. When you're handling the rock of life in your hands, you have to find ways to feed that hunger. You do what you love, especially when it's hard. No matter the pain, no matter the suffering, you push through to pursue something righteous and meaningful. And in that pursuit, you find the intelligence, the clarity, and the direction to make a real impact in the lane you're driving in. *That* is mental toughness. The battle is never-ending. You'll fight against darkness your entire life, but the goal is to keep finding the light. Not just during hard times, but during good times too. Because when you can find the light no matter the circumstance, *that's* when you are truly at your best.

When you develop light and it's burning within you, you've built something I call a heavenly muscle. If you're not religious, maybe you just call it peace. It's a calm feeling in the middle of chaos, a quiet presence inside you that doesn't get shaken so easily anymore. Whatever you call it, it's powerful. That light, that peace, that muscle isn't built physically. It's built from the intuitions and feelings of a warm and invisible connection we can't see. It's not something we create on our own. It's born out of darkness. It's born from struggle, from disappointment, from moments that test us to the core. That's what gives us the chance to master this feeling of heavenly strength we try to hold on to every single day. And it's what led me to one of the greatest books I've ever read and one I still turn to when life tries to knock me off course: *The Anatomy of Peace* by the Arbinger Institute.

This book is life-changing. It helped me see something we all deal with, something the book calls "the box." Every one of us ends up in that box at some point. It's the place where we only see the world through our own eyes, our own pain, our own justifications. We believe our story is the only one that matters. We convince ourselves we're right and everyone else is wrong. We play the blame game. We defend our choices with a fake kind of righteousness that might feel good at that moment but ultimately hurts the people around us and hurts us even more. And the worst part? It doesn't actually fix anything. The injustice we feel doesn't go away. The pain doesn't disappear. It sits with us and grows inside of us unless we make the choice to see things differently. The box becomes a claustrophobic and suffocating mental cage. It keeps us stuck in hate, animosity, jealousy, pride, and in all the things that keep us from becoming who we are truly meant to be. It breaks you down, piece by piece, until you lose sight of the light you worked so hard to build.

Seeing Through Another's Eyes

This book is like the Bible when it comes to learning how to see the world through someone else's shoes. Literally. There's a part in *The Anatomy of Peace* where a teenager, staying at a rehabilitation center, was struggling to cope with dealing with relationships, emotions, and pain they couldn't manage. One day, the teen tried to escape. At this particular center, students were allowed to wear shoes, even though the staff knew some had tried to run away before. I have experienced this before so I could definitely relate. This moment in the book reminded me of when I worked at a group home for troubled teens in my college days where kids could only wear their shoes at certain points of the day, so they limited them the chance to run away. This story reminded me of those experiences, and I was pulled into this story. In this teen's moment of desperation, overwhelmed by the darkness inside, this teen found a way to slip away. This teen bolted through the forest and desert of Arizona, in the middle of the heat at over 100 degrees. Not a smart decision, but when you're deep in darkness, you'll do anything to out-run the light, especially when you don't believe it can actually help you.

    Most in this situation as a staff would have responded with force or panic, but instead, they made a different choice. Rather than send an overwhelming search party, they chose two staff members to quietly go after the teen, not to overpower them, but to protect them. And here's the part that stopped me in my tracks. As these staff members would catch up to the tired teen, the teen would take off again and again until a certain stoppage when—this time the teen lost their shoes and started to run with no shoes on—the staff voluntarily took off their shoes and started the chase without theirs. They ran barefoot after that teen through the brutal Arizona terrain because they wanted to show this kid they were in it with them. That they weren't just chasing, they were walking (and running) through the same pain. The pursuit lasted for hours. Every time they got close, the teen would run again. But the staff didn't give up. They stayed the course, running not just with their feet, but with empathy. Eventually, the teen gave in, exhausted and broken down by the relentless love and patience that was chasing them. By the end of it, all three of them were bruised, cut, and burned. But the connection they gained was something far deeper.

Why would those workers do that? It goes back to the idea of being "in the box." How can you truly understand desperation if you've never experienced it or even tried to imagine what it looks or feels like? A teenager caught in emotional turmoil will go to great lengths, sometimes even hurting themselves, to escape a situation they believe is trying to fix something they don't believe is broken. In their mind, there is no problem. Pain is the norm for them.

Those workers, by taking off their shoes and running barefoot through the Arizona desert, stepped outside of their own boxes. They didn't sit in judgment or comfort. They entered into the struggle, literally and figuratively. Now they know what desperation looks like. They know what it feels like to run toward someone else's pain, not away from it. That experience, raw and difficult as it was, gave them the empathy to understand how far someone will go when they are mentally hurting. And when you understand that, you're no longer just a bystander and you become part of the healing.

Lesson #5 – Read the Words from the Greatest Minds

Energy Vampires: Don't Be Your Own Enemy

This short story is just a story within the story, as the book itself centers on a father who is a former military man who runs a company that's falling apart. He's losing employees, profits are down, and while trying to hold it all together, he's also trying to raise a defiant teenage son. Their relationship is strained, to say the least. The father wants his son to eventually take over the company, but the son is spiraling down the wrong path. Out of frustration and desperation, the father takes his son to a rehab center, thinking the place is just for troubled youth. But what he doesn't realize is that the center isn't just meant to help the kids, it's just as much for the parents. Through this journey, the father discovers that the real problem isn't only with his son, it's also within himself and within their family. The powerful message of the book is that we are often trapped inside the box of our own distorted views, assumptions, and emotional walls. We don't see ourselves clearly, and we certainly don't see others clearly either. The story of the barefoot chase through the desert is the perfect metaphor for getting outside that box. It taught me that true understanding comes when we're willing to step into someone else's pain, and when we stop judging from afar and start living with more compassion.

Without a story like this, I may have never been able to understand the process of not only working through my own grief and pain but also being able to view pain through the eyes of someone else. If this story unfolded right in front of your eyes without knowing the background, you'd probably say, "That kid is crazy." And yes, running barefoot through the desert in 100-degree heat is extreme. But once you understand the deeper reason behind the action, your whole perspective shifts.

Empathy doesn't erase the behavior, but it allows us to be more patient with people who are hurting. It opens our eyes to the root of their pain, rather than focusing only on the reaction. The wisdom we gain through stories like this gives us a wider lens through which to view our own shortcomings as well as the shortcomings of others. Learning from peers, mentors, authors, even celebrities who've walked difficult roads, helps remind us that no one is exempt from struggle. Everyone has their "box," their blind spots, their moments of darkness. And anyone, no matter how well-known or unknown, can offer insight and light that helps you find your way. Every experience is a tool to guide us toward healing. And the earlier you begin building this mental awareness, the more equipped you'll be to handle the rock later in life when the pressure rises and the stakes are even higher.

These words from the books I've read and the ones I've written are meant to give you courage. I hope that, by reading this chapter, the words you discover will spark resilience within you and help you recognize that you *do* have a purpose, and you *will* find it. The right words from the voices you trust and resonate with your heart, have the power to unzip your soul and expose it to the peace and grace it's been yearning for. When those words align with your passion and purpose, something inside of you wakes up. Even if you've never met the person who spoke or wrote those words, a connection forms. It's unspoken, but it's powerful.

We see it all the time. People adore celebrities, authors, or athletes they've never met, not because of proximity, but because of the way these people live, speak, and carry themselves. Their words and actions create an invisible thread of inspiration. Maybe they'll never know the impact they've had on someone else's life. But here's the thing: as you're reading *my* words, the same kind of connection is happening. You picked up this book for a reason. Maybe the title spoke to something inside you. Maybe you saw yourself in one of these stories. Maybe you're realizing that we share a journey in some way. But you wouldn't

Lesson #5 – Read the Words from the Greatest Minds

know that unless I chose to write this all down and created a record of my truth through these words.

Every page, every sentence has been written with the belief that someone like you would read it and be moved to take action, to grow, to fight, and to *live*. Writing isn't easy. Sticking with it hasn't been easy. But knowing that my words might reach someone who needs them? That makes it worth every second. This is my legacy. It's not about fame or accolades; it's about impact. I want you to be stronger because of this. I want you to fight whatever you're going through with more belief, more grit, more hope. I might never see your growth firsthand, but I believe in it. I believe in you.

We have to rid ourselves of being our own worst enemy, our own energy vampires. We need to learn how to ride the waves of life without sinking. It starts early and it starts in the mind. I don't want to see another child, another good person, slowly destroy themselves with thoughts they think they can't escape. I've been there. I know how deadly those thoughts can be. I've lived with them. I've felt the suffocation of a mind trapped in its own darkness, a coffin of thoughts that feels impossible to break free from. But I'm here to tell you … it *is* possible. You *can* beat that death in the mind. You *can* win this war between your ears. And when you do, you'll know what it means to have an Empire State of Mind.

Keep the Waters Flowing

Once you become free from the negative thoughts that try to bury your mind, you unlock something powerful: a free spirit with wings that let you rise above the heaviness and discover more than just surface-level success. You begin to tap into the deeper, richer parts of life. You find joy, not because everything is perfect, but because your inner character is calm, focused, and no longer at war with itself. That calmness and peace becomes your fuel. They replace the sadness that once lingered in the shadows.

One of my favorite coaches of all time is Coach K from Duke University. He recently retired after more than 40 years of coaching college basketball. A legend. A leader. A teacher. He once said, "If you hear it, you'll forget it. If you see it, you'll remember it. If you do it, you'll understand it." That quote stuck with me and is why I'm writing this and why I hope you don't just read these words, but you apply them. Once you put this book down, I urge you to do something with what you've learned. Don't let it sit. Don't let it fade. Take action. Move. Practice.

Because when you take the words that resonate with you and you start *doing* them, that's when real transformation begins. The more you hear from voices that uplift you, the more you see people living with passion and purpose, the more you'll want to take those actions for yourself. You won't copy them. Instead, you'll build upon them in your own way, using their wisdom as your foundation. That's the beauty of reading the words from the greatest minds, from the past and in the present. Their words can shape your greatness, but only if you *do* something with them.

The key to greatness is to stay on this path for your entire life. Never stop your willingness to listen, to see, and to do. That's the process. That's the foundation of an Empire State of Mind. That's what it means to handle the rock. There's always room for growth. I think of our lives as rivers. There's always a source where everything begins. From that starting point, the water flows, moving through different paths, sometimes quietly, sometimes with force, until it hits an edge that has a drop off that creates a breathtaking waterfall. The water crashes, continues, and then flows again. As the river flows, every twist and every fall of the river's journey gives life. That water sustains everything it touches.

Lesson #5 – Read the Words from the Greatest Minds

But here's the truth: if something disrupts that flow, like a beaver building a dam, a fire scorching the land, or if humans interfere, the entire ecosystem feels the loss. Life that depended on that flow begins to wither. And isn't that just like life? We are born with a source inside us, a current of purpose, of energy, and of light. It may not always seem linear, and the path might feel random, but when we're in flow and our spirit is aligned, we move beautifully through the world. Then something happens. A loss, a betrayal, a setback, someone or something builds a dam in our path and the flow gets blocked, the water slows down, and sometimes it even stops. The source is still there, but it's no longer feeding the life it once nourished.

That's why we have to keep our waters clean. Keep the energy flowing. Feed your life with positivity. Fuel it with growth. Protect your source. When we do this consistently, we build something unstoppable like the river that created Niagara Falls. Constant, powerful, majestic, and it's a force that cannot be tamed. So, when trials come—and they will—they'll barely make a ripple in your waters. Why? Because you've created momentum that's fed daily by intentional learning, having self-belief, and mental toughness.

You are the source. You are the flow. And as long as you keep feeding that source with the right energy, good knowledge, strong values, and meaningful connections, no obstacle can divert your course for long. There's always room to grow, to stretch your mindset, to expand your reach, and to pour more life into those around you. An empire is built by making sure our waters never stop moving.

I never read much while growing up, but now I wish I had. I'm grateful that I eventually discovered the gift of wanting to read and learn from the words of the greatest minds. It took a long time for that desire to be planted and grow within me, but now that it has, I cherish it. I'm grateful that I not only found it, but that I now have the ability to share it with others like you. I've felt the power that comes from learning through words. I've gained strength knowing that if others could overcome, lead, rise, and thrive, then so can I. Without the history written in books, captured on social media, and passed down in the stories told by those closest to us, I would've never fully realized the power of this tool we all have at our fingertips. Without those shared teachings, I wouldn't have had the voice, clarity, or ability to articulate what I've been able to express in this book. That's what handling the rock is truly about.

Throughout this book, I've used basketball as the thread to weave together all of these lessons, hoping to show you what mental toughness really looks like. And I hope you've not only read about it, but felt it, as you've walked through the stories I've shared from my life. Basketball has taught me more than how to play a game. It's given me a lifetime of lessons. It's been a mirror, a teacher, and a gift. Through it, I've had countless opportunities to develop my mental toughness and discover who I truly am, not just as a player or coach, but as a man.

Every situation in my life I can relate back to an end-of-game scenario in basketball. Because just like life, there's tension, stress, joy, disappointment, and a whole process that unfolds before you ever see the final result. The end of a game has so many intangibles that make it unforgettable, whether you're on the winning or losing side. If you can imagine playing in an arena filled with thousands of fans, lights blaring, and a deafening crowd screaming at levels your ears can barely handle, it all plays a role in how you handle the moment. You and your teammates are in a back-and-forth battle, like a boxing match, exchanging haymakers on every possession. Neither team can pull away. Every possession demands everything from you fighting through screens, sprinting the full length of the court, playing physical, trying to stop your opponent from scoring or creating a shot

Lesson #5 – Read the Words from the Greatest Minds

for their teammate. Every foul feels harder, every free throw has the weight of the world on it, and the tension is so thick you can feel it in the air with every breath.

Then, the game comes down to a final possession. Ten seconds on the clock. You're down by one. You race the ball up the court and your coach calls a timeout. This is it. You huddle with your team, and you look around into your teammates' eyes. There's a singular focus, but underneath, you can tell some are nervous, some are calm. A lot is on the line.

Coach pulls out the whiteboard and draws up a play. Everyone is locked in, communicating their roles. Coach stays intense, but calm, because he knows too much tension will break you. You can barely hear one another over the noise, but the play is simple: a pick-and-roll on the left wing with your two best players. After the screen, the roller down-screens for your best shooter to pop out to his favorite spot—the left wing—for a wide open shot. It's not a complex play with a million moving parts. It's simple, clear, and everyone understands it.

Meanwhile, the other team is huddled on their end, drawing up their counter. Maybe they'll switch the screen, maybe deny the shooter, maybe foul. They're talking through it just like you are. Both sides are preparing for the same moment, but only one team is going to come out on top. The question is, who will it be? Who's going to break under pressure? Who's going to rise up and execute? Moments like these don't just reveal skill; they reveal mental toughness. They expose who's been preparing for these moments and who's pretending. It's not about the play. It's about the mindset. This, right here, is what it means to handle the rock. This is mental toughness in motion.

I can tell you this: these moments are never easy. Whether it's in the game of basketball or in the game of life, the outcomes we experience are usually determined long before the big moment arrives. Why, you ask? Because the lessons you've learned are what prepare you to either win or lose in those moments.

In life, just like on the court, you'll face situations where a single decision could change everything. It may not happen in front of a packed gym full of thousands, but it could happen in front of one person (even in a quiet moment with yourself) where you must choose whether to rise or fall. That's where your foundation matters. That's when your Mecca, your vision, your culture, and your sacrifice all show up. The nights you stayed in while others partied, the consistency in holding yourself accountable when you missed a day of workouts or went when you didn't want to go and using the strength to turn your adversity of losing something important to you into a gift, all of it matters.

Every bit of effort, every ounce of discipline, every detail you paid attention to becomes your weapon in these pressure-filled moments. That's what it means to handle the rock. This Empire State of Mind helps you perform when everything's on the line.

I've coached teams that hit game-winners with .9 seconds left after trailing by 20. I've seen our defense lock down an opponent in the final possession to seal a win. I've watched my own kids hit game-winning shots. I've hit a game winning shot. And yes, we've lost too. I watched a player foul with one second left in a tie game to lose a game. I have been up by 20 points and lost the game. As mentioned, I shot a shot in the wrong basket at 12 years old and should have known better. I have been on both sides of this fence. They are both hard to deal with in their own way. The work it takes to win is painful. To take a loss when you give everything you have is painful. Winning and losing always has a price. Sometimes it feels more expensive in different situations. Overall, it's excruciating work when you want something bad. You can't win every competition, but you most certainly have to win in your mind every day to keep moving with purpose. We need to face

Lesson #5 – Read the Words from the Greatest Minds

these head on and to handle the rock. In any case of our lives, when work meets preparation, you will compete and understand the outcome as it comes.

Winning isn't just about the scoreboard. It's about being mentally and emotionally ready to face the moment head-on whether you win or lose. These lessons are the playbook and when you embed them into your life, good things will follow. Even when things fall apart, you won't. Because your mind is strong enough to keep going. You'll find yourself calm in chaos, able to respond with clarity, and grounded in your truth. That's hitting the game-winner in life.

Borrow from the wisdom of great men and women but make it yours. Let it live through your actions. No one wants to suffer, but everyone will at some point. Some seasons of pain will pass quickly. Others may feel like they last forever. But you get to decide how you learn, how you grow, and how you handle it.

These lessons are your guide and your compass. They're your counterattack to despair, confusion, and hopelessness. Life is filled with detours. It's unpredictable, like driving through New York City with all its traffic, potholes, noise and chaos. With an Empire State of Mind, you'll absorb those distractions and obstacles with poise. You'll navigate through it all. You'll handle your rock like a pro.

Your existence matters. You are loved. If you aren't loved by anyone else, then know you're loved by me. These words are proof of that. So, take these lessons, build your power, claim your mental strength, and live with intention. You have the power. You have the will. You now have—and will always have—your own Empire State of Mind.

Now go out and handle the rock.

Conclusion

Building Your Empire, One Thought at a Time

You've now journeyed through the stories, strategies, and soul of what it means to embrace an *Empire State of Mind*—a mindset built on courage, conviction, and the commitment to rise above limitations.

This book has not just shared ideas; it has invited you into the minds of action takers, visionaries, and everyday warriors who chose to stand tall despite the storms. They didn't wait for perfect timing or flawless plans. They moved. They built. They believed.

And now, it's your turn.

Your empire doesn't have to look like anyone else's. It starts with a single decision to think differently, to act boldly, to believe that your story matters, and that your life is worth building with intention and impact.

The *Empire State of Mind* is about grit and hustle and, most importantly, it's about rising with purpose, staying grounded in truth, and expanding your influence not for ego, but for legacy.

So, whether you're just laying the foundation or you're adding to the skyline of your dreams, remember this:

Conclusion

You are the architect. You are the builder. You are the empire.

Now go out there and rule your world with your newfound Empire State of Mind.

~Coach Khalil "Puddy" Sikander

About the Author

Khalil "Puddy" Sikander, a former Utah SHAPE High School Physical Education Teacher of the Year and Basketball Coach of the Year with over 20 years of experience as an educator and coach, wants to leave a legacy beyond a game.

As a leader on the basketball court, educator and now business owner of a youth program, he has made it a goal to use his experiences in life as an adult and child to share his story of how and what it means to be mentally tough. With his love of helping people, Khalil has stayed the course with his vision to become a successful 3x bestselling author, speaker and entrepreneur so this vision can continue to be fulfilled.

Khalil never planned to be an author, yet life challenges have given him the strength to put the lessons learned through his adversity into a book that will last the tales of time. His dream was always to become a professional basketball player but learned some dreams don't come true but other dreams can come to life from failures and hardships of past dreams that were not accomplished. Khalil's mental toughness journey is a testament of that.

Whether he was handling the rock on the court or handling life's toughest blows, Khalil's journey is living proof that resilience, inspiration, and true mental toughness are built one hard-fought

About the Author

moment at a time. From his childhood living in the mud of poverty while dealing with the dirt of adult experiences, Khalil will help you find your mental strength as he takes you through his mental toughness journey. His story will help you become mentally fortified.

Connect with Khalil at khalil@utahbasketballclub.org

www.ingramcontent.com/pod-product-compliance
Lightning Source LLC
Chambersburg PA
CBHW070451100426
42743CB00010B/1580